# An Early Start to Poetry

## Colin Walter

**Consultant Editor**
**Roy Richards**

Macdonald Educational

Introduction and compilation © Colin Walter 1989
Artwork © Simon & Schuster 1989

First published in Great Britain in 1989 by
Macdonald Educational
Simon & Schuster International Group
Wolsey House, Wolsey Road
Hemel Hempstead HP2 4SS

8|7|89

Printed in Great Britain by
Purnell Book Production Ltd

British Library Cataloguing in Publication Data

Walter, Colin
   An early start to poetry.
   1. Great Britain. Primary schools.
   Curriculum subjects: Poetry in English.
   Teaching
   I. Title II. Richards, Roy
   372.6′4

ISBN 0-356-16046-7

Series Editor: **John Day**
Editor: **Carolyn Jones**
Designer: **Jerry Watkiss**
Production: **Rosemary Bishop**

ILLUSTRATIONS

Cover illustration: **Bob Harvey***

**Paul Bonner***: 21, 43, 60-61
**Robert Cook***: 34, 64-65, 67
**Marilyn Day***: 20, 30, 42, 58, 63
**M. C. Escher:** 51
**Sharon Gower***: 23, 36, 38, 40, 52-53, 56, 70-71
**Bob Harvey***: 16-17, 31, 72-73
**Edward Lear:** 49
**Jon Miller***: 18-19, 26, 28, 29, 32, 37, 59
**Fraser Shaw***: 54-55
**Jerry Watkiss:** 35, 44-45
**Dan Woods***: 24-25, 46

*Represented by David Lewis Illustration Agency

DEDICATION

I am obliged to, and wish to thank, the following who have contribu
in various ways to this book.

The staff and children of South Park Junior School, Redbridge, for a
year's worth of welcomes into their school; in particular Eileen
Campbell and Peter Drewe, the school's head teacher, for their end
patience and support. John Loveday for many insights into, and
conversations about, poetry for children. Michael Rosen for agreein
my using Corrine Willson's 'The Sulk'. Finally, Cheryl, Joanne and
Emma for never sulking when I disappeared for the evening – nor
when I came back!

**Colin Walter**

# An Early Start to Poetry

# Contents

# Teachers' Introduction

A sympathy for poetry begins very early in life. Babies find pleasure in playing with sound even before they start to speak; thereafter, many parents use songs and rhymes to entertain their children and to help them learn about living. Poetry in school can and should build on this foundation.

Poetry, like the other arts, has an important role to play in helping children to understand themselves and the world. We do it, and them, a disservice if our poetry teaching is haphazard or misdirected. To teach poetry effectively we need an approach which is thorough and based on sound principles.

Our approach, or teaching plan, must meet a number of requirements. It must be as suitable for a multicultural class of children as for a class who have a common ethnic background. It must be able to support the development of a poetry curriculum for children from the age of five to eleven; however, it must also be relevant to a class of nine- or ten-year-olds who have not previously experienced coherent poetry teaching. Further, our methods should take account of the different time-scales over which children are influenced by their experience with poetry. Some effects will be apparent immediately. Some will appear gradually over a period ranging from one year to the full six years of primary education.

So, how should we begin? We cannot teach poetry well unless we recognize that the human fondness for poetry has both individual and social origins. Therefore, we should promote right from the start all the ways in which children can become involved with poetry: listening, reading in private, reading in public (silently or aloud) and composing. If we support children's activity in all these areas, we will help poetry to enter both their public and private lives. By these means, they will also learn to recognize the variety of forms and subjects embraced by the term 'poetry'. Our chief aim is to support children in becoming active and interested readers and makers of, listeners to and enquirers about poetry. We may count ourselves successful if they become committed, in the long term, to being any one of these. However, children who love reading poetry usually enjoy writing it, and so on.

To be successful, our teaching methods must recognize the two principal influences on children: first, their attachment to rhyming, song and chant in the playground; second, their activities as readers and writers in school. We should think, too, about the relation between the two activities of reading poetry and writing it. This relation expresses for children, just as it does for mature poets, the necessary tension between what we 'inherit' and what we 'make for ourselves'. Without doubt, much of young children's writing gains from the rhythms, sounds and syntax of nursery and playground rhyme. Yet, also, what they read and hear read to them influences their composing. A particularly appealing poem may inspire children to write about similar subjects. In the same way, the forms and structures that children meet as readers gradually influence the way they shape their own poems. This is a slow process, however.

Listening and telling dominate children's playground lives. So, in school we introduce children comprehensively to being readers and writers of poetry by using their existing and developed abilities as listeners and tellers in play situations. Our priority is to introduce children to the literate culture of poetry as quickly as possible.

# The Beginning of Children's Reading and Composing

We can measure our success in teaching by how quickly children read poetry for pleasure and from choice. All our planning should be directed at getting children to read poetry habitually. Making poetry a normal part of their reading activity in the classroom is important at every stage of children's development as readers, but it is only a part of the means we can use to support children as readers of poetry.

The case is the same for their writing. When children 'choose' to make poems as writers they will treat the writing process as continuous throughout their waking lives; this is exactly what mature poets do. Working on a poem in the classroom as part of mainstream writing activity is only a part of the wider process of making a poem. Further, children's commitment to the activity of writing in class has several origins, just as their commitment to reading does.

We need to know how to start out when encouraging children to write, and how to support them once they have begun. Our methods must take account of the fact that the meaning of a poem comes slowly to the reader, or rather it does not come all at once. With children it is particularly evident that the enthusiasm for reading a poem is derived from a commitment to re-reading it; this is so for private reading and for reading aloud to companions. Much of the pleasure of reading lies in the knowledge that we can re-read. Therefore we are wise if we try to harness children's love of collecting to their developing interest in poetry. The action of writing out a poem for which they have already discovered a liking, in order to save it, helps its meaning to come. Our teaching methods must recognize this, as they must the influences of the social world of childhood, the influence of the teacher as model, and the parental encouragement that children of these years often receive when they take their enthusiasms home from school.

When children write habitually, reviewing their experiences and organizing them into poetry, they often say that the reason they enjoy writing is that it enables them to preserve or remember something (see page 73). Their willing approach to composing poems, including their choice of subject, is readily explained when we note the similarity of the activity to their play as much younger children at home. Both offer a means of ordering and understanding life experience.

Children have little trouble in understanding that the making of a poem occurs over a period of time and that working upon it is necessarily threaded in and out of many other activities in and out of school. They have to be supported in fitting their classroom writing into a larger pattern of working. It is important to establish a framework for developing children's writing of poetry through the primary school years. It would not be overstating the case to claim that success in the classroom depends upon what the teacher has actively encouraged and planned to occur 'between' lessons.

We can ensure that poetry becomes an important and valued childhood activity, so that our children come to the classroom well informed about the relevance, satisfactions and processes of reading and writing poems. Although children's output and interest in composing will vary, and for periods of time they may prefer reading or listening, it is possible to ensure that by the time they are eleven they have a sense of having made a number of different kinds of poems.

Children often become fiercely committed to composing poems. As they do so, what they say reveals just how poetry acquires for them a private and a social importance. Their activity as writers depends equally upon their private inner worlds and their social worlds of brothers and sisters, peer group, parents, grandparents and teachers. While their writing is influenced by what they read and hear when their peers or teachers read aloud, it is also rooted in a social world outside the classroom. In the classroom we should not overlook how their commitment to writing is influenced by hearing day by day how their own experience as writers is paralleled by that of friends and classmates.

Reading is the major way that children inherit the poetry of the distant and recent past which is relevant to their lives. Their commitment as readers and writers often proceed together. For instance, children often choose to write within the forms of poems which they have previously read or heard (although they are not necessarily conscious of what they are doing). This process is indeed no more than an extension of what occurs in oral play with rhyme, chant, joke and song in the playground. There, also, they inherit forms from the past and yet in re-making rhymes they bring in their own particular experience of the contemporary world. Children's love of parody, so often demonstrated in playground life, is potent evidence of this interest and ability in adopting and renewing inherited forms. (Some examples of children's parodies are included in the anthology on pages 18 to 19.)

# Getting Started

## 1 Building a collection

Assemble as many selected author collections and anthologies suitable for the age of the children as you can. (Two books per child is the ideal starting point: it *is* possible.) Before long a further collection will be necessary from which to supplement and replace the first books distributed. It is essential, therefore, to liaise with the school library service and the local authority's resource centre, and plan to have access over the first term to as many volumes as possible. A bibliography is provided at the back of this book which contains the titles of over 100 collections that children have enjoyed.

## 2 Private reading

As you first distribute the books, two to a child (if possible), explain that these books are for private reading at school or at home. At the same time, give them an empty writing book in which to write out any poem which they particularly enjoy and wish to save. Stress that they should only write in poems which they particularly like. Ask them to include the author's name, the title of the book in which the poem was found, and the date they found it. Ask the children to exchange the books with each other as soon as they have finished with them. It is prudent, of course, to check periodically just who currently holds each title, and how far the process of exchanging has progressed in order to prepare for partial or complete renewal of the books.

## 3 Reading aloud

After a week, spend about half an hour, or forty minutes for older juniors, with children reading aloud to the group poems which they have discovered. This is best done with half the class at a time to encourage a relaxed and intimate atmosphere, while the other children do something equally absorbing. At this stage it probably will be necessary to remind the children to write out the poems which they enjoyed either in reading or listening. This collecting and writing out of poems should occur between sessions to avoid loss of time in the meetings, which should take place weekly.

Thus, soon after they have begun to read poems in private and select favourites for presentation, all the children in the class start to read poems aloud in public and listen to others' reading. Although it is important that the two groups should meet weekly, there may also be occasions where it is appropriate for the whole class to work together. The important thing is that the activities of pleasurable private reading, collecting, selecting, public reading and listening should be established and maintained.

The set-piece opportunities for public sharing quickly encourage, and in turn are supported by, numerous patterns of informal sharing and interaction between special friends in pairs, or very small groups of children, as they reveal to each other what they have found. This occurs both inside and outside the classroom and is initiated entirely by the children.

## 4 Starting to write

Very soon some children will ask if they may try their hands at writing their own poems. It really is worthwhile letting the request come from them, for you will seldom have to wait long. When it happens, you can ask the children to put their completed poems, along with the date of completion, into their personal collections. Stress that only completed poems should be included.

If they choose, their own writing may then become part of the established activity of presentation to the group, along with poems chosen from private reading. Alternatively, writers may choose only to show their work to a few friends, just to you as a teacher, or to no-one. Although it is important always to allow these options to the children, most primary children present their work publicly with great enthusiasm. In most cases the awareness that they will have an audience of their own age for their writing becomes part of the process of composition.

You, the teacher, have now established all the contexts, both private and public, of children's involvement with poetry. They are able to work precisely as mature poets work. You can fit your own public contribution, as chooser and presenter of poems, into the children's activities. In addition, do not overlook the importance of teachers trying to be writers too among writers; it is no bad thing to have one or two suitable poems of your own to hand for when a child asks to hear a poem by you.

All these activities should be well established before the end of the first three weeks of the school year. The books in circulation to support private reading activity should be supplemented by books which the children borrow from the school, class and public libraries. Your role in bringing poems to read aloud from favourite personal books remains of great importance. You will find that your children become increasingly keen to buy books of poems and to seek them as presents from parents, friends and relations. There are many low-cost and high-quality paperback volumes of poetry for children on the market and, in the context of the teaching strategies described, children will perceive it as desirable to own them and bring them to school.

## 5 A visiting poet

The activities described so far should be continued and developed during the whole of the first two terms. At the beginning of the third term it will be time for a poet to visit the school to work with the children in writing workshops. Of course, arrangements for this must be made well in advance, perhaps before the start of the school year.

There are a number of poets who are very skilled teachers of young children in school, and enlisting their help may be inexpensive or quite free. It is possible that you may be able to approach the poet of your choice directly. Alternatively, there are two easy means of arranging for a poet to join you in your work. The *Writers in Schools* scheme administered by the regional arts associations pays half the poet's fee along with travelling expenses. At the time of writing, the full daily fee is £70. The other scheme to provide a poet is administered by the *Poetry Society*. It is sponsored by W. H. Smith Plc, and is entirely free to schools. In addition to giving details of the scheme, the Poetry Society provides a valuable national Information Service for children, along with a separate one for teachers (see page 76). Once contact has been established between school and poet, both are free on succeeding occasions to enter into their own arrangements.

A suitable pattern for the workshops which ensures an immediate impact on the children and which, if fees are paid, is very economical, is three consecutive weekly visits by the poet lasting a whole afternoon. Whatever arrangements are selected, ensure that the workshops run very early in the summer term to allow plenty of planning time between you and the visitor. This will also enable you to develop the work done in the workshops during the remainder of a long term. The children will be able to bring to the workshops informed contributions and, not least, a good body of writing already achieved, for they will already have become apprenticed to making what poets make.

## How Children's Commitment to Poetry in School Develops

### Private and public reading
The children will begin to read poetry privately at home and in other contexts outside the classroom but in school, as well as in the classroom. This variety of contexts for private reading encourages the re-reading of poems.

Working in a full range of contexts, children will begin to apprehend the immense variety of forms of, and subjects for, poetry. Extensive private reading is an important means of inheriting the poetry of the past.

Children's reading will begin to include the writing of classmates. In addition, their private reading and re-reading of their own work will begin. They will start to read their own work for the purpose of revising and redrafting it as part of the process of composition.

Public reading aloud of poems will begin to occur in all the contexts in which children read privately. When primary children find pleasure in something they have discovered, they want to share it with parents and family in the home, with other relatives, and with friends. They will choose those audiences closest to them: poetry will become part of the junior-aged child's peer group relationships.

As pleasurable reading becomes habitual, in a number of different places, the poems which children select from their private reading to read aloud to the group in school will have been shared already with family and friends. Thus children will have experienced the responses and support, the enjoyment and endorsement of their choices from a range of audiences, both adult and children. In this way the child's choosing of a poem comes to entail a great deal more than merely bringing a poem to the classroom to read aloud. With that poem comes not only the original reasons for the child's attraction to the poem but a network of social and cultural exchange which has already contributed to the child's understanding. In an important sense, therefore, the poem which reaches the child as a result of his/her involvement in a literate culture, in fact now exists in the same kind of cultural relationship to the child as does the playground rhyme. The significant difference is that adults are endemic to the activities of reading and writing whereas in the child's playground life they are necessarily absent.

### Composing poems
The children will write just as working poets do, choosing their own subjects and their own place and time of writing. They will write in a variety of situations, whenever seems most appropriate.

They will become aware, because they will feel it happening, that fashioning language into a poem is usually a slow process, requiring revision and redrafting. It will become apparent that the processes of making a poem do not usually result from acting on the proposition 'today I will write a poem'. Rather, they are achieved in the many nooks and crannies of daily life and do not run to a timetable.

As children become regular writers they will begin to realize that the poems that they read and hear influence the shape and content of their own writing. Talking with others about poetry, they will also perceive that everyday language in play or conversation may also offer its rhythms to a poem.

Children will begin to share with companions a common emergent understanding of the processes of writing. Their pleasure in and understanding of composing will be confirmed as they recognize that their companions' efforts reflect their own. They will see that their writing is influenced by what they hear of companions' discoveries. Similarly, they may to a greater or lesser extent recognize how their own poems influence the writing activity of companions in the group.

The informal audiences which support children's reading will just as surely support their composing activity. The responses of parents, relations and friends become part of the writing process and influence the making of the poem.

When our teaching encourages children to bring their own reading and composing activity to the classroom, their poetry 'lessons' may endorse and inform their commitment as young readers and writers. Our success as teachers depends on our enlisting every child's potential interest in poetry, rather than concentrating on classroom activities immediately or exclusively. We must seek to keep together the public/social and the private/internal aspects of a commitment to poetry. Thus, when children come to consider poetry in the school curriculum in the public arena of the classroom, the meeting will not be a confrontation. Our teaching methods will recognize and enlist children's implicit understanding of the ways and means of poetry, rather than ignoring or affronting it. We will have protected the sources of success in the classroom.

We can best introduce children to a literate involvement with poetry by drawing on the potency of their intimate and informal social lives, halfway between their private selves and the wider culture of school. The contexts of this 'intermediate' cultural life are the very same ones in which the children in our classroom once played in early song and nursery rhyme, and the same that now support playground chant, rhyme and song.

## The Poetry Table

The poetry table has two principal purposes: to support and develop children's private and public reading of, listening to and writing of poetry; and to encourage children's involvement with poetry outside the classroom as well as in it.

All your skills of visual presentation should be lavished on this resource. Select as large a table or surface as you can, with adjoining display areas. (You can attach additional display areas to the front of the table as required.) Give the table a title in bold and attractive lettering.

Plan the introduction of the table as a pleasant surprise. Time spent assembling it at the end of school one afternoon will make it possible to have the table ready when the children arrive the following morning.

### Making and using the table

Initially the table will consist of a small number of carefully selected author collections, assembled by you. It is a good idea to type out an example of a poem which you are sure will appeal to a large number of the children, and mount it centrally on the display area behind the table.

Once the children express interest in the table, suggest that they bring in their own books from home to leave on it on a daily basis. Encourage them to use the table as a source for private reading activity, both for set reading periods and individually on occasions when other classroom activities are completed. By agreement, they may borrow books and take them home for return the following day (or as decided).

As the resource becomes established, the books will be a focus of informal public sharing between friends and groups of children. Encourage the children, at times, to supplement these informal reading exchanges by reading poems they have discovered to the whole class at the very moment when their surprise and pleasure are freshest.

The books on the table should be changed as you judge appropriate. It is useful to keep a record of new titles as they are published. As the term goes on, it is valuable if children agree to leave their own personal collections on the table.

There will be many occasions when you will bring in your own books containing poems which you intend reading to the class or to the groups. It is worthwhile to leave them on the table beforehand. To appear always to go to the table as a source of enjoyable activity, and to 'select' a book, demonstrates to the children the value of the poetry table. For the same reason a book should be replaced when you have finished reading from it, if only for a short while.

The table is a tangible way of demonstrating to your children the close relationship between their composing and their reading activity. Thus it is useful for supporting their writing specifically. Individuals may choose to leave on the table either collections of their own poems or individual poems. With their agreement, and where it seems appropriate, you may choose to type examples of children's work for presentation. Gradually, therefore, your children learn to look to the table for their companions' poems, which then become subject to informal reading and interest just like poems found in books.

There will be many opportunities to use the poetry table in a flexible way to encourage your children to read each other's poems with sensitivity and interest. It is important that children should not think that they are required to offer publicly everything, or anything, they write. Children develop as writers at varying rates, and the value of what is made is not to be measured by the speed of its production. Some children may prefer to seek only a small audience of immediate friends. Some may wish to offer it to you first. The ways, means and degrees of children first seeking an audience for their work are many and varied. It is important that we allow them to make their own decisions. We want them to work as poets work: to choose their subject and their audience. This is integral to the whole business of effective poetry teaching. We should try to reproduce the conditions which allow children to make poems in an authentic, individual and spontaneous way.

You may find the poetry table a useful support in presenting yourself (in a low-key way) as a writer. When children find a few examples of your own poems on the table, the point of their composing is further confirmed without impossible demands being placed upon your abilities as a writer. This also removes the possibility of your poems becoming prescriptive to the children in ways you would not wish.

## What appears on and around the table?
◇ Books brought by you.
◇ Books the children bring.
◇ The children's personal collections of poems they have read and written out to 'save'.
◇ Carefully-typed poems selected from any of the above to emphasize excellence or achievement.
◇ Variously arranged small collections of items from children's writing compiled by you and the children. Also typed single poems.
◇ Posters and leaflets advertising poetry events which the children have attended or may attend.
◇ Any other suitable item of interest about poets and poetry, past or contemporary.

# Getting a Wider Audience

Towards the end of the first term the volume of the children's selections from their private reading and listening will be substantial. The whole class will be used to selecting and reading aloud favourite poems, both found and written, and they will be well on the way to becoming habitual listeners. Privately, they will have become regular readers and re-readers. Both specific poems and the activities already described will have become part of the children's everyday lives.

The children will have become increasingly aware that they regularly consult a number of people both in and out of school as they read and write, listen and tell. Now the time has come to extend formally the audience for what the children are doing. In the second and third terms you may usefully arrange the following events to promote further the children's understanding of, and commitment to, poetry:

### Reading to another class
Ask the children to choose two or three poems which they have really enjoyed reading, and some examples of their own writing with which they are satisfied. In this way you can compile a programme to be read to another class in the school. Adjust your demands if necessary to suit the progress of individual children; it is never a bad thing to arrange for a few reserve items.

A large part of an afternoon should be put aside for the event and both classes should be given plenty of notice of it. It is best to choose, for an audience, children who are near in age to those doing the readings. The atmosphere of the event should be as informal as practicable, and the children should expect to talk about their selections in response to questions and comments from the audience, which should be encouraged to participate.

Each member of your own class should be responsible for choosing their own items for the event which you should conduct on the day. As you will anticipate, much of the preparation for their reading will be executed by the children in out-of-class situations; in educational terms this is most desirable for the reasons already described.

### An evening with parents and friends
This is the next logical and enjoyable way to extend the range of audiences in school for the children's work, and to make new learning demands upon the class. As mentioned earlier, parents and other people who are part of the home life of the children will have long been involved in many ways with pupils' reading and writing activity. Now that hitherto unseen audience comes together as a public audience to the reading and composing of the whole class. This will further promote in an enjoyable way those learning activities and processes out of school by which children become active readers and composers, choosers, tellers, presenters and listeners.

The evening will have the further value of acting indirectly upon the children's own perceptions of what they have been doing since the beginning of the year, both in and out of school. At the end of the evening parents and children may be reminded of the next event.

### An evening with a poet and children's writing
On this evening at the very end of the school year, parents and friends will return to hear a presentation by the children of writing which they achieved during the writing workshops run by the visiting poet. All of these poems, produced in an anthology, should be available for everyone to take away and the children should be involved in the selection of the poems. A supporting programme of music and children's introductions and commentary to thread together the evening's items may be arranged quite

easily. It is likely that the poet will agree to run the evening. As previously, the evening should be as informal and relaxed as is practicable, for it should be a kind of celebration.

### Reading to a class in another school
At any time towards the end of the summer term, a visit may be made to a class of children of the same age in a neighbouring school, to present a programme of readings as described earlier.

## School initiatives to support classroom work

Agreements among the whole staff may result in initiatives which support classroom work in several important ways. Among these are the following:

◇  The building of a long-term relationship between the school and one or two poets so that children become accustomed to seeing them around.

◇  The attendance by ten- and eleven-year-olds at the week long residential courses run by the Arvon Foundation at its two centres in Devon and Yorkshire (see page 76). Here, in rural settings, working poets guide children in their writing.

◇  Visits of groups of children to half-day local events which bring together poets, poetry, teachers and children. The invaluable service to teachers and children of the Poetry Society, and the work of the regional arts associations will keep you informed of forthcoming readings and local workshops for children of primary school age. Another useful organization providing reviews, information, news and a publication called *Poetry Express* is the Schools' Poetry Association based in Winchester (see page 76).

## This Anthology

The following anthology is for private reading and public sharing. It is intended for private reading by both children and teacher. It is also meant to be a source of material from which the teacher may select to read to the class.

Some of the illustrations in the anthology refer to children's work in other areas of the curriculum for which poetry has provided the starting point or inspiration. These serve as a reminder of the special opportunities we have in the primary school to help children make explicit connections between different kinds of creative activity.

Some of the poems are composed by children. With the exception of 'Grandma' by Susan Boughtwood, all of these were written during one year's work in a multicultural London school.

When offering the poems of established poets, a balance has been sought between the contemporary and the long dead. The poems have in common that each has been offered in excitement by a child either to me, or to other children in my hearing in a classroom. I am confident, therefore, that Byron's 'She Walks in Beauty' is as relevant to children's interests as Mary Ann Hoberman's 'Brother'.

The selection attempts to encourage the full range of children's imaginative potential and predilections as readers. Children's tastes are as much represented, I believe, by the idea of grandparents being 'old and grey and full of sleep' as by that of throwing eggs at grandmother's legs! We have as much of an obligation to offer to children the stark experience and truths of the two poems by Vernon Scannell as the gentle subversiveness of Michael Rosen's 'Chivvy.' All of these, along with many others, represent aspects of childhood experience,

and even sometimes preoccupations; no one of them is the whole story nor will each speak equally clearly to all children. Indeed, the fact that they may not is a reason for being eclectic, and as comprehensive as prudent, when choosing poems to 'present' to children. Children have many tastes during the primary school years. One of these is for the world they know to be confirmed, and their perceptions of the world are, in the main, celebratory. The realization that threatening experience is a part of their own and others' lives and may be recognized and faced, may itself become a cause for celebration. This, too, is part of the fun of poetry.

This collection has at least one recurrent theme, and that is the relationship between adult and childhood life, as represented for instance in the recognizable actions of adults. The fascination for children of this relationship, and their ability within specific conventions to address it, is closely connected with a main focus in the theory of poetry teaching which has been outlined: the connection between what children inherit and what they make for themselves. This scenario exists in the playground, too, where they add their own contributions to the traditions in rhyme and play which they inherit from other children.

During the primary school years, while possessing an individual voice and an individual view, a child's relation to the inherited traditions both literary and social is still characterized by dependency. Although this is a transitional state, it is important for us to help them grasp the opportunities of this period of relative harmony, in order that later they may move to approach the genuine tension between form inherited and form made that is felt by mature poets.

This anthology seeks to parallel the journey made by children as they become enthusiastic about poetry from books. They travel from the spoken to the written and back; from early song and playground rhyme to the book; from public to individual involvements and thence to a different order of public involvement, and so on.

It would be pleasant to hope that the collection might serve as a convenient symbol for the importance of recognizing the origins of our pleasure and skills as listeners to and tellers of poetry, and their importance to children becoming committed to reading and composing poems. The earliest pages of this anthology are intended as a reminder of those origins.

A number of poems are included which, I think, are themselves a celebration of what poetry is and what it has to offer, because they represent a certain fineness which adult and child can recognize although they will perceive it differently. You may choose to read these aloud to the children as part of that reciprocal process of choosing and presenting which has been emphasized. It will, naturally, be necessary for you to prepare the children by some discussion and consideration of the human contexts into which the poems fit.

The powerful first impression of a poem may well depend upon the power of specific lines which enter ears and minds still receptive to the songs and chants of the playground, and from this beginning grow within the aural sensibilities of children. So children's attachment to a poem, to what it is and how it works, may begin with the glamour of a line and then become informed and develop upon their memory that 'The fair breeze blew, the white foam flew/The furrow followed free.' They may know at ten, yet recall at who knows when in their future, that there are 'huge and mighty forms that do not live/like living men'. Now, as later, they will recognize someone who 'walks in Beauty like the night/of cloudless climes and starry skies'. Just because of the words, alone, children may understand better a time of year 'When weeds, in

wheels, shoot long and lovely and lush.' And, a little, a time of life 'When you are old and grey and full of sleep.' As such lines echo in their memories children understand well enough where such effects of the sound of these ordinary words in combination come from. They will understand at this stage more than they are able, or should be asked, to explain. Simon shows he understands these origins when he ends his poem 'Up the Stairs' on page 57 with the line 'I always jump the last step'. All children show how they understand when they laugh at the parent's chiding line 'no-one thinks you're funny', in Michael Rosen's poem.

As well as expecting children to be attracted to some poems by the resonance of a few of their lines, we should anticipate their interest in the preoccupations and realities of adult life. There is no clearer confirmation that children of these years have both the skill and the motivation to handle the facts of the human condition than the eight-year-old Susan Boughtwood's poem on page 69. Entirely from choice and from the resources of her own language she builds into an object made from words the recent loss of her grandmother.

The anthology ends with children talking about their composing, as earlier they talked about their reading of poetry. Everything quoted was said in a classroom by the children whose poems are included in the anthology. The conversations are a tiny selection of recordings made over a year. I am sure that the reasons for including these few words from the children about how they see poetry will be clear to the reader. Equally, I am certain that as you interpret the first principles of poetry teaching which I have attempted to isolate, you will collect richer confirmation still of the ability of children in the primary school to make poetry a part of their lives. In teaching poetry, as in all teaching, the quality of our beginning holds the key to our later successes.

**Colin Walter**

# I Cannot Give The Reasons

I cannot give the reasons,
I only sing the tunes:
the sadness of the seasons
the madness of the moons.

I cannot be didactic
or lucid, but I can
be quite obscure and practic-
ally marzipan

In gorgery and gushness
and all that's squishified.
My voice has all the lushness
of what I can't abide

And yet it has a beauty
most proud and terrible
denied to those whose duty
is to be cerebral.

Among the antlered mountains
I make my viscous way
and watch the sepia fountains
throw up their lime-green spray.

*Mervyn Peake*

## Playground rhymes and songs

Eena, meena, mina mo,
Catch a tiger by the toe,
If he squeals let him go,
Eena, meena, mina mo.

Not because you're dirty
Not because you're clean
My mother says
You're a wicked old queen
The one who comes to number ten
Will surely not be it
2 4 6 8 10 you're out
Not because . . .

Sea shells, cockle shells,
Eevy, ivy, over.
Mother's in the kitchen
Doing a bit of stitching.
How many stitches can she do?
10, 20, 30 . . .

Eeny, meeny, miney mo,
Sit the baby on the po,
When he's done
Wipe his bum
Tell his mummy what he's done.

Mother made a seedy cake,
Gave us all the belly ache,
Father bought a pint of beer,
Gave us all the diarrhoea.

Teddy bear, teddy bear,
Turn around.
Teddy bear, teddy bear,
Touch the ground.
Teddy bear, teddy bear,
Climb the stairs.
Teddy bear, teddy bear,
Say your prayers.
Teddy bear, teddy bear,
Turn out the light.
Teddy bear, teddy bear,
Say G-O-O-D-N-I-G-H-T.

Two, four, six, eight,
Mary's at the cottage gate,
Eating cherries off a plate,
Two, four, six, eight.

Dip, dip, dip,
My blue ship,
Sailing on the water,
Like a cup and saucer.
Dip, dip, dip,
You are not it.

Hands together
Eyes closed
Teacher has
Big toes

## Parodies

Mary had a little lamb,
It had a sooty foot.
And everywhere that Mary went,
Its sooty foot it put.

I scream, you scream,
We all scream "Ice-cream!"

### FRED FERNACKERPAN
#### A Mystery Goblin

Roses are red
Violets are blue
Most poems rhyme
But this one doesn't

I am a mystery fellow,
    I'm Fred Fernackerpan,
I wear one sock that's yellow
    The other dipped in jam.
I walk about the countryside
    I walk about the town,
Sometimes with my trousers up
And sometimes with them down:
And when they were up they were up
And when they were down they were down
And when they were only half way up
    He was arrested.

*Spike Milligan*

Hickory Dickory Dock
Three mice ran up the clock
The clock struck one
One mouse ran down
And the other two escaped with minor injuries

Little Miss Tuckett
Sat on a bucket
Eating some peaches and cream;
There came a grasshopper
And tried hard to stop her;
But she said,
"Go away, or I'll scream."

Just one Cornetto
Give it to me –
You must be joking
It's 50p

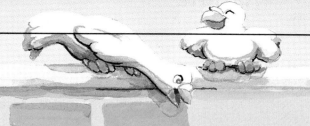

Apples are red
My nose is blue
Standing at the bus stop
Waiting for you

Humpty Dumpty sat on a wall,
Humpty Dumpty had a great fall;
All the King's horses
And all the King's men said,
"Oh no, not scrambled eggs for breakfast again!"

Roses are red
Violets are blue
I was born pretty
What happened to you?

Humpty Dumpty sat on a wall,
Humpty Dumpty had a great fall;
All the King's horses
And all the King's men
Trod on him.

Humpty Dumpty sat on a wall,
Humpty Dumpty had a great fall;
All the King's men didn't know
what to do,
So one went back for the superglue.

Kisses spread germs
So it's stated.
Kiss me baby
I'm vaccinated.

Humpty Dumpty sat on a wall,
Eating blue bananas,
Where do you think he put the skins?
Down the King's pyjamas!

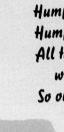

**Do you know any more?**

## Baby's Drinking Song

*for a baby learning for the first
time to drink from a cup*

Sip a little
Sup a little
From your little
Cup a little
Sup a little
Sip a little
Put it to your
Lip a little
Tip a little
Tap a little
Not into your
Lap or it'll
Drip a little
Drop a little
On the table
Top a little.

*James Kirkup*

## This is the Key

This is the key of the kingdom:
In that kingdom there is a city.
In that city there is a town.
In that town there is a street.
In that street there is a lane.
In that lane there is a yard.
In that yard there is a house.
In that house there is a room.
In that room there is a bed.
On that bed there is a basket.
In that basket there are some flowers

Flowers in a basket.
Basket in the bed.
Bed in the room.
Room in the house.
House in the yard.
Yard in the lane.
Lane in the street.
Street in the town.
Town in the city.
City in the kingdom.
Of the kingdom this is the key.

*Anon*

## Brother

I had a little brother
And I brought him to my mother
And I said I want another
Little brother for a change.

But she said don't be a bother
So I took him to my father
And I said this little bother
Of a brother's very strange.

But he said one little brother
Is exactly like another
And every little brother
Misbehaves a bit he said.

So I took the little bother
From my mother and my father
And I put the little bother
Of a brother back to bed.

*Mary Ann Hoberman*

## Magic Word

"More jam," said Rosie to her Mom.
"I want more jam," said she.
    But no one heard
    The Magic Word.
Mom took a sip of tea.

"The jam! The jam! The jam!" she cried.
Her voice rang loud and clear.
    "I'd like to spread
    It on my bread."
But no one seemed to hear.

"*Please* pass the jam," Rose said at last.
Now *that's* the thing to say.
    When Mother heard
    The Magic Word
She passed it right away.

*Martin Gardner*

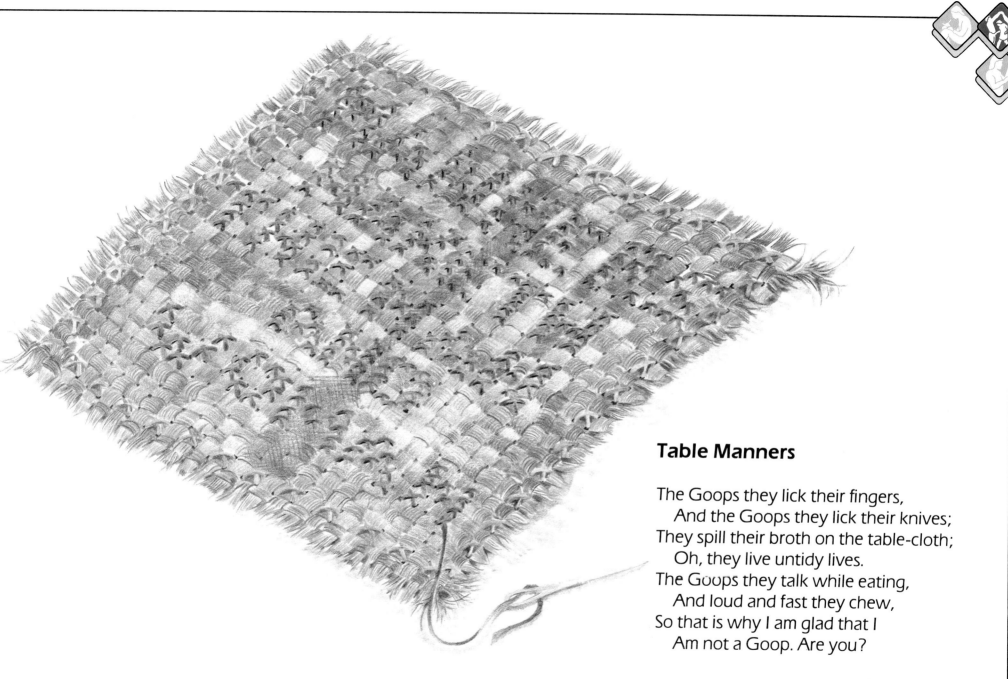

## Table Manners

The Goops they lick their fingers,
   And the Goops they lick their knives;
They spill their broth on the table-cloth;
   Oh, they live untidy lives.
The Goops they talk while eating,
   And loud and fast they chew,
So that is why I am glad that I
   Am not a Goop. Are you?

Gelett Burgess

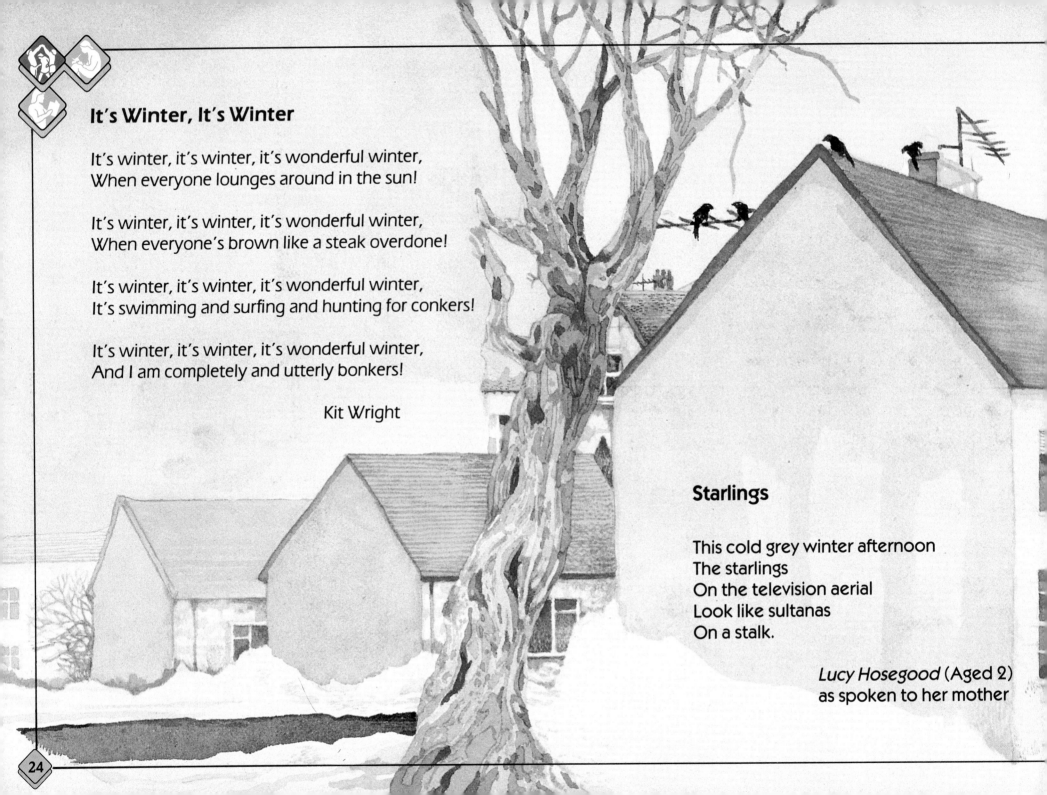

## It's Winter, It's Winter

It's winter, it's winter, it's wonderful winter,
When everyone lounges around in the sun!

It's winter, it's winter, it's wonderful winter,
When everyone's brown like a steak overdone!

It's winter, it's winter, it's wonderful winter,
It's swimming and surfing and hunting for conkers!

It's winter, it's winter, it's wonderful winter,
And I am completely and utterly bonkers!

Kit Wright

## Starlings

This cold grey winter afternoon
The starlings
On the television aerial
Look like sultanas
On a stalk.

*Lucy Hosegood* (Aged 2)
as spoken to her mother

I saw a lady with red hair
talking to one with blue on

the sun shone
and the rain ran
the streets emptied
the people had gone

when I looked
for the ladies again
there was a purple stream
flowing down the drain

Michael Rosen

## The Kitten

The trouble with a kitten is
THAT
Eventually it becomes a
CAT.

*Ogden Nash*

From:

## The Adventures of Isabel

Isabel met an enormous bear,
Isabel, Isabel, didn't care;
The bear was hungry, the bear was ravenous,
The bear's big mouth was cruel and cavernous.
The bear said, "Isabel, glad to meet you,
How do, Isabel, now I'll eat you!"
Isabel, Isabel, didn't worry,
Isabel didn't scream or scurry,
She washed her hands and she straightened her hair up,
Then Isabel quietly ate the bear up.

Once in a night as black as pitch
Isabel met a wicked old witch.
The witch's face was cross and wrinkled,
The witch's gums with teeth were sprinkled.
"Ho, ho, Isabel!" the old witch crowed,
"I'll turn you into an ugly toad!"
Isabel, Isabel, didn't worry,
Isabel didn't scream or scurry,
She showed no rage, she showed no rancour,
But she turned the witch into milk and drank her.

Isabel once was asleep in bed
When a horrible dream crawled into her head.
It was worse than a dinosaur, worse than a shark,
Worse than an octopus oozing in the dark.
"Boo!" said the dream, with a dreadful grin,
"I'm going to scare you out of your skin!"
Isabel, Isabel, didn't worry,
Isabel didn't scream or scurry,
Isabel had a cleverer scheme;
She just woke up and fooled that dream.

Whenever you meet a bugaboo
Remember what Isabel used to do.
Don't scream when the bugaboo says "Boo!"
Just look it in the eye and say, "Boo to you!"
That's how to banish a bugaboo;
Isabel did it and so can you!

BOOOOOO to you.

*Ogden Nash*

## A Little Girl I Hate

*I saw a little girl I hate*
*And kicked her with my toes.*
*She turned*
*And smiled*
*And KISSED me!*
*Then she punched me in the nose.*

Arnold Spilka

# Eletelephony

Once there was an elephant,
Who tried to use the telephant —
No! no! I mean an elephone
Who tried to use the telephone —
(Dear me! I am not certain quite
That even now I've got it right.)

Howe'er it was, he got his trunk
Entangled in the telephunk;
The more he tried to get it free,
The louder buzzed the telephee —
(I fear I'd better drop the song
Of elephop and telephong!)

*Laura E. Richards*

## The Sulk

I'm in a sulk
An angry sulk.
Can't have an ice cream.
It's not fair —
Mum says I ain't allowed to have an ice-cream
For a whole week,
Imagine that, no ice-cream
For a whole week.

I'm in a sulk.
An angry sulk.
Can't play out.
It's not fair —
Mum says I ain't allowed to play out
For a whole week
Imagine that, no playing out
For a whole week.

I'm in a sulk.
An angry sulk.
Can't play me organ.
It's not fair —
Mum says I ain't allowed to play me organ
For a whole week.
Imagine that, no playing me organ
For a whole week.

Can't do nuffin' in this 'ouse.

*Corrine Willson* (Aged 9)

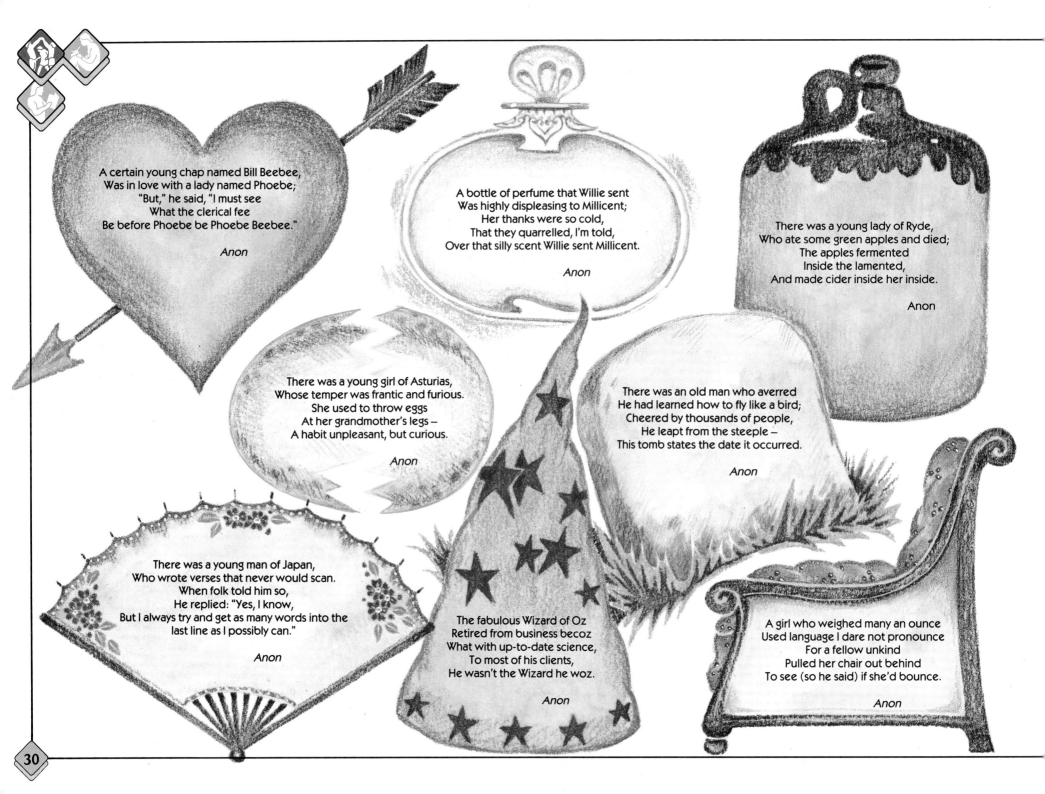

A certain young chap named Bill Beebee,
Was in love with a lady named Phoebe;
"But," he said, "I must see
What the clerical fee
Be before Phoebe be Phoebe Beebee."

*Anon*

A bottle of perfume that Willie sent
Was highly displeasing to Millicent;
Her thanks were so cold,
That they quarrelled, I'm told,
Over that silly scent Willie sent Millicent.

*Anon*

There was a young lady of Ryde,
Who ate some green apples and died;
The apples fermented
Inside the lamented,
And made cider inside her inside.

*Anon*

There was a young girl of Asturias,
Whose temper was frantic and furious.
She used to throw eggs
At her grandmother's legs —
A habit unpleasant, but curious.

*Anon*

There was an old man who averred
He had learned how to fly like a bird;
Cheered by thousands of people,
He leapt from the steeple —
This tomb states the date it occurred.

*Anon*

There was a young man of Japan,
Who wrote verses that never would scan.
When folk told him so,
He replied: "Yes, I know,
But I always try and get as many words into the
last line as I possibly can."

*Anon*

The fabulous Wizard of Oz
Retired from business becoz
What with up-to-date science,
To most of his clients,
He wasn't the Wizard he woz.

*Anon*

A girl who weighed many an ounce
Used language I dare not pronounce
For a fellow unkind
Pulled her chair out behind
To see (so he said) if she'd bounce.

*Anon*

## Talking about reading poetry

"I like to collect what I like. Everything seems fun then — it gives you a bit of an arm-ache each night."

"Well, I was ill a few days ago. So I was lying in bed and I had nothing to do so I picked up this poetry book you lent me, it was really great."

"Yes, I read them to my family to see what they think"

"Linda let's hear the one about your hospital visit."

"I read some poems again and again."

"I'd mind if there was no poetry, it's short and doesn't go on and on. I like it because it's short."

"I read them to myself and then I read one to my mum."

"Mm, I read them to myself and I read them to my friend, and I read them to my sister, and then we start laughing."

## Dead and Alive

And in my dreams I sometimes see
a brontosaurus tracking me
with lashing tail and tiny head,
but I'm alive and he is dead.

He swam to many funerals
of other scaly animals,
but now he's turned to ribs of stone
and only left behind one bone.

*Leonard Clark*

## My Hospital Visit

I walked into hospital
As shaky as can be.
I was just in time for dinner
With roast beef and veg...

The day I went in was Sunday,
Monday was the operation day.
I went to bed that night,
As sleepy as can be.

I woke up the next morning
And had a bath at twelve.
The operation was at one o'clock,
I was not a bit nervous.

The time came for the injection in bed
That was just to make me sleepy
They pricked me in the leg with a needle.
Mmmm what a nice feeling!

I went to sleep for an hour
Until one o'clock came.
They said to me, "Wake up, Wake up
It's time to have the op...."

They wheeled me on the bed of wheels
As I left my mum that time.
She said she'd come back in the evening
To see how I was getting on.

I was in the room at last, at last,
Where the operation was to take place.
They pricked a needle in my arm
And I quietly dozed to sleep.

I woke up at three o'clock,
Thinking it wasn't done.
I raised my head and looked above
And watched the nurse's smile.

They wheeled me back into my ward,
And everyone said, "Hello!"
They also said, "How did it go?"
I answered, "I don't know."

Night soon came.
Most people were asleep.
The doctor came to see me,
To see how I was.

Morning came and we had our breakfast,
Just as we normally do.
"The nurse said I can come home today!"
That was alright I thought.

The afternoon came, and I had to go home,
"Bye Bye Bye."
I said goodbye to the nurses and bye to
   the patients
With a sigh, "Goodbye".

Linda Huff (Aged 9)

## Rain

I opened my eyes
And looked up at the rain
And it dripped in my head
And flowed into my brain
So pardon this wild crazy thing I just said
I'm just not the same since there's rain in my head.
I step very softly
I walk very slow
I can't do a hand-stand
Or I might overflow.
And all I can hear as I lie in my bed
Is the slishity-slosh of the rain in my head.

Shel Silverstein

## The Months

January cold desolate;
February dripping wet;
March wind ranges;
April changes;
Birds sing in tune
To flowers of May,
And sunny June
Brings longest day;
In scorched July
The storm-clouds fly
Lightning-torn;
August bears corn,
September fruit;
In rough October
Earth must disrobe her;
Stars fall and shoot
In keen November;
And night is long
And cold is strong
In bleak December.

*Christina Rossetti*

# Questions, Quistions & Quoshtions

Daddy how does an elephant feel
When he swallows a piece of steel?
Does he get drunk
And fall on his trunk
Or roll down the road like a wheel?

Daddy what would a pelican do
If he swallowed a bottle of glue?
Would his beak get stuck
Would he run out of luck
And lose his job at the zoo?

Son tell me tell me true,
If I belted you with a shoe,
Would you fall down dead?
Would you go up to bed?
— Either of those would do.

*Spike Milligan*

Where do pineapples grow?
I don't know!
Do they grow on a tree?
Search me!

*Simon Vincent* (Aged 9)

## Parrot

Sometimes I sit with both eyes closed,
But all the same, I've heard!
They're saying, "He won't talk because
He is a *thinking* bird."

I'm olive-green and sulky, and
The family say, "Oh yes,
He's silent, but he's *listening*,
He *thinks* more than he *says*!

"He ponders on the things he hears,
Preferring not to chatter."
— And this is true, but *why* it's true
Is quite another matter.

I'm working out some shocking things
In order to surprise them,
And when my thoughts are ready I'll
Certainly *not* disguise them!

I'll wait, and see, and choose a time
When everyone is present,
And clear my throat and raise my beak
And give a squawk and start to speak
And go on for about a week
*And it will not be pleasant!*

*Alan Brownjohn*

## Yogurt Pots

You open your packed lunch box
And things are looking black.
Your wife has not put in your malt-loaf
You ask for Sunday back.
Things look even glummer
When you find that you have got
A little bit of foil on a pesky yogurt pot!

The yogurt pots they spit and spurt,
The tabs are even worse,
You twist, and turn, and tug them,
To try to get them loose.
And finally you get the tab
Level with the top!
You pull so gently upwards, then —
Oh! What a flop!
It's torn off!

Those little bits of foil on those pesky
YOGURT POTS!

Simon Vincent (Aged 9)

# My Dad, Your Dad

My dad's fatter than your dad,
Yes, my dad's fatter than yours:
If he eats any more he won't fit in the house,
He'll have to live out of doors.

*Yes, but my dad's balder than your dad,*
*My dad's balder, O.K.,*
*He's only got two hairs left on his head*
*And both are turning grey.*

Ah, but my dad's thicker than your dad,
My dad's thicker, all right.
He has to look at his watch to see
If it's noon or the middle of the night.

*Yes, but my dad's more boring than your dad.*
*If he ever starts counting sheep*
*When he can't get to sleep at night, he finds*
*It's the sheep that go to sleep.*

But my dad doesn't mind your dad.
*Mine quite likes yours too.*
I suppose they don't always think much of us!
*That's true, I suppose, that's true.*

*Kit Wright*

## The Tale of Custard the Dragon

Belinda lived in a little white house,
With a little black kitten and a little grey mouse,
And a little yellow dog and a little red wagon,
And a realio, trulio, little pet dragon.

Now the name of the little black kitten was Ink,
And the little grey mouse, she called her Blink,
And the little yellow dog was sharp as Mustard,
But the dragon was a coward, and she called him Custard.

Custard the dragon had big sharp teeth,
And spikes on top of him and scales underneath,
Mouth like a fireplace, chimney for a nose,
And realio, trulio daggers on his toes.

Belinda was as brave as a barrel full of bears,
And Ink and Blink chased lions down the stairs;
Mustard was as brave as a tiger in a rage,
But Custard cried for a nice safe cage.

Belinda tickled him, she tickled him unmerciful,
Ink, Blink and Mustard, they rudely called him Percival,
They all sat laughing in the little red wagon
At the realio, trulio, cowardly dragon.

Belinda giggled till she shook the house,
And Blink said "Weeck!" which is giggling for a mouse.
Ink and Mustard rudely asked his age,
When Custard cried for a nice safe cage.

Suddenly, suddenly they heard a nasty sound,
And Mustard growled, and they all looked around.
"Meowch!" cried Ink, and "Ooh!" cried Belinda,
For there was a pirate, climbing in the winda.

Pistol in his left hand, pistol in his right,
And he held in his teeth a cutlass bright,
His beard was black, one leg was wood;
It was clear that the pirate meant no good.

Belinda paled, and she cried "Help! Help!"
But Mustard fled with a terrified yelp,
Ink trickled down to the bottom of the household,
And little mouse Blink strategically mouseholed.

But up jumped Custard, snorting like an engine,
Clashed his tail like irons in a dungeon,
With a clatter and a clank and a jangling squirm,
He went at the pirate like a robin at a worm.

The pirate gaped at Belinda's dragon,
And gulped some grog from his pocket flagon,
He fired two bullets, but they didn't hit,
And Custard gobbled him, every bit.

Belinda embraced him, Mustard licked him,
No one mourned for his pirate victim.
Ink and Blink in glee did gyrate
Around the dragon that ate the pyrate.

But presently up spoke little dog Mustard,
"I'd have been twice as brave if I hadn't been flustered."
And up spoke Ink and up spoke Blink,
"We'd have been three times as brave, we think,"
And Custard said, "I quite agree
That everybody is braver than me."

Belinda still lives in her little white house,
With her little black kitten and her little grey mouse,
And her little yellow dog and her little red wagon,
And her realio, trulio little pet dragon.

Belinda is as brave as a barrel full of bears,
And Ink and Blink chase lions down the stairs;
Mustard is as brave as a tiger in a rage,
But Custard keeps crying for a nice safe cage.

*Ogden Nash*

# I Saw a Jolly Hunter

I saw a jolly hunter
   With a jolly gun
Walking in the country
   In the jolly sun.

In the jolly meadow
   Sat a jolly hare.
Saw the jolly hunter
   Took jolly care.

Hunter jolly eager —
   Sight of jolly prey.
Forgot gun pointing
   Wrong jolly way.

Jolly hunter jolly head
   Over heels gone.
Jolly old safety-catch
   Not jolly on.

Bang went the jolly gun.
   Hunter jolly dead.
Jolly hare got clean away
   Jolly good, I said.

*Charles Causley*

# In Bed

When I am in bed
I hear
footsteps of the night
sharp
like the crackling of a dead leaf
in the stillness.

Then my mother laughs
downstairs.

*Charlotte Zolotow*

# Somebody Said That It Couldn't Be Done

Somebody said that it couldn't be done –
But he, with a grin, replied
He'd not be the one to say it couldn't be done –
Leastways, not 'til he'd tried.
So he buckled right in, with a trace of a grin;
By golly, he went right to it.
He tackled The Thing That Couldn't Be Done
And he couldn't do it.

*Anon*

# Little Old Man

Little old man hunched and grey
I know you were young once – like me.
But it's hard to believe I'll ever be
the way I see you are today
hunched and grey,
little old man
(once young like me)

*Charlotte Zolotow*

# How Strange

How strange when I finally die
to lie beneath the grass and snow
while overhead the birds fly by
and I can't watch them go.

*Charlotte Zolotow*

## What's for Tea?

I said, "What's for tea?
Maybe apple pie and cream
Or chocolate mousse with two or three cherries.
Could it be chocolate ice-cream with hazel nuts?
That's what I think is for tea."

Joey said, "I wonder what's for tea?
Maybe a giant knicker bocker glory.
Or orange flavoured jelly with soda-pop?"
That's what Joey thinks is for tea.

Simon said, "I wonder what's for tea?
Maybe jam tarts and whipped cream.
Or cookies and cold lemonade?"
That's what Simon thinks is for tea.

Mother says, "I'll tell you what's for tea.
Fruit cake and a cup of tea.
No fancy treat!
That's what you will get for tea!"
Said mum, angrily.

*Anjuna Dharni* (Aged 9)

## The Check-up

The dentist says, "Don't eat sweets,
It's very bad for your teeth.
Chewing gum and liquorice sweets,
Chocolate and caramel sweets."
That's what the dentist said to me.

My mum said to me, "Don't eat sweet things,
It's very bad for your teeth.
Like ice buns and cream cakes.
Ice cream cornets and cream cake tarts."
That's what my mum said to me.

One day my mum said to me,
"Hello, Hello, what's this? Let's see."
When she opened the strange letter she pulled out
A white card.
"It's an appointment for the dentist,
We have to go tomorrow."

I never expected this at all.
I shivered with fear, and said, "Oh dear!"
The next day I didn't feel that good.
Mum said, "Don't be silly, it's only a check-up!"

*Anjuna Dharni* (Aged 9)

## What Has Happened to Lulu?

What has happened to Lulu, mother?
　What has happened to Lu?
There's nothing in her bed but an old rag-doll
　And by its side a shoe.

Why is her window wide, mother?
　The curtain flapping free,
And only a circle on the dusty shelf
　Where her money-box used to be?

Why do you turn your head, mother,
　And why do the tear-drops fall?
And why do you crumple that note on the fire
　And say it is nothing at all?

I woke to voices late last night,
　I heard an engine roar.
Why do you tell me the things I heard
　Were a dream and nothing more?

I heard somebody cry, mother,
　In anger or in pain,
But now I ask you why, mother,
　You say it was a gust of rain.

Why do you wander about as though
　You don't know what to do?
What has happened to Lulu, mother?
　What has happened to Lu?

Charles Causley

# Chivvy

Grown-ups say things like:
Speak up.
Don't talk with your mouth full
Don't stare
Don't point
Don't pick your nose
Sit up
Say please
Less noise
Shut the door behind you
Don't drag your feet
Haven't you got a hankie?
Take your hands out of your pockets
Pull your socks up
Stand up straight
Say thank you
Don't interrupt
No one thinks you're funny
Take your elbows off the table

Can't you make your *own*
mind up about anything?

*Michael Rosen*

# Children's Questions

### 1 *Julian, 4*

We follow down the turning stair
Into a room far underground,
Regard the scratched stone walls, sense fear
And horror grained on every inch.
"If you will keep your children near,
I'll put the light out, so you'll see
How dark it was." A switch somewhere
Imprisons us. The dungeon's dark
Is absolute. Silenced, we hear
The nothing prisoners heard, watch for
The glimmering that should appear
When eyes have grown accustomed. Close,
A child whispers, "Are we still here?"

### 2 *Marina, 10*

"How do we know," the child asked, "that
We're not dreaming all this?" — meaning
The world, our whole experience.
Ten years of living shaped the thought;
Ten more have hidden what I said.
Perhaps it was, "The world seems real."
"Perhaps our dreams are real," she said.

*John Loveday*

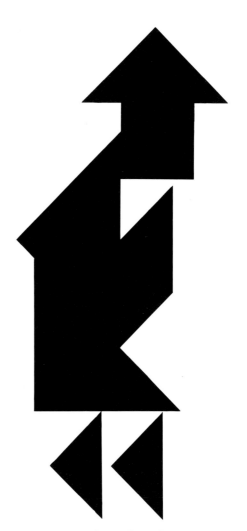

## Psychological Prediction

I think little Louie will turn out a crook. He
Puts on rubber gloves when stealing a cookie.

Virginia Brasier

## The Well

"You'll never bring him up, my dear:
That vein across his little nose –
A sign he'll drown."
                          The coverlet,
The pillow, and the small face blurred.
She held the handle hard, the pram
Her only anchor in a world
In flood. "I'm sorry, dear, to tell
You this, but that's a sign."
                          Then she
Was walking home, old Biah gone,
Her crow's garb gone, her white face gone,
Her words not gone, never to go.

You dropped a stone in, and the sound
Came up a long time afterwards,
A cold sound, dark, that frightened you
To make you look and drop again.
Lean over far enough, and far,
Far down, a face looked up at you.
You broke it with a stone.

The pail went lolloping down, banging
The dark green sides, until it tipped
And sank. You wound it up slowly,
Not to spill. There was another way.
Let go, the iron handle spun,
The chain raced off the roller and
The pail fell straight. After the jerk,
The chain was tight, down there the pail
Suspended still. Winding, you looked
For its coming back, the glimmering
About to break the surface, felt
Something like welcome for it when
It spilt its silver round the rim.

How long is "bringing up"? she wondered
As the years passed, watched the vein,
Less noticeable as boyhood came.
Was there a time beyond which all
Harm's ways were barred? the pond outside
The door, the well, the summer sea,
And all the unknown places dared
In urchin hours? Tom scoffed, but built
A wooden structure on the well,
With bolted door. "These bloody old
Wives' tales." But some were sometimes true.

In time, the bolt stayed drawn, the door
Even lay open carelessly.
(Once, a rat was found, floating,
The water left untouched for days.)
The curious stones dropped in, and soon
The pail, wound on a chain of trust
In what was normal for a boy –
Who did not drown.

               Disused for years,
The well has been filled in, rubble
And soil have proved it shallower
Than a boy's imaginings.
He'll not drown here.
                      The vein still shows,
The more when tension comes, though five
Decades have gone. He wonders sometimes if
Old Biah had the superstition wrong,
If some dark water waits him still.
The hand that held the pram will never know.

*John Loveday*

# The Jumblies

## I

They went to sea in a Sieve, they did,
   In a Sieve they went to sea:
In spite of all their friends could say,
On a winter's morn, on a stormy day,
   In a Sieve they went to sea!
And when the Sieve turned round and round,
And everyone cried, "You'll all be drowned!"
They called aloud, "Our Sieve ain't big,
But we don't care a button! We don't care a fig!
   In a Sieve we'll go to sea!"
     Far and few, far and few,
      Are the lands where the Jumblies live;
     Their heads are green, and their hands are blue,
      And they went to sea in a Sieve.

## II

They sailed away in a Sieve, they did,
   In a Sieve they sailed so fast,
With only a beautiful pea-green veil
Tied with a riband by way of a sail,
   To a small tobacco-pipe mast;
And everyone said, who saw them go,
"O won't they be soon upset, you know!
For the sky is dark, and the voyage is long,
And happen what may, it's extremely wrong
   In a Sieve to sail so fast!"
     Far and few, far and few,
      Are the lands where the Jumblies live;
     Their heads are green, and their hands are blue,
      And they went to sea in a Sieve.

## III

The water it soon came in, it did,
   The water it soon came in;
So to keep them dry, they wrapped their feet
In a pinky paper all folded neat,
   And they fastened it down with a pin.
And they passed the night in a crockery-jar,
And each of them said, "How wise we are!
Though the sky be dark, and the voyage be long,
Yet we never can think we were rash or wrong,
   While round in our Sieve we spin!"
     Far and few, far and few,
      Are the lands where the Jumblies live;
     Their heads are green, and their hands are blue,
      And they went to sea in a Sieve.

## IV

And all night long they sailed away;
   And when the sun went down,
They whistled and warbled a moony song
To the echoing sound of a coppery gong,
   In the shade of the mountains brown.
"O Timballoo! How happy we are,
When we live in a Sieve and a crockery-jar,
And all night long in the moonlight pale,
We sail away with a pea-green sail,
   In the shade of the mountains brown!"
     Far and few, far and few,
      Are the lands where the Jumblies live;
     Their heads are green, and their hands are blue,
      And they went to sea in a Sieve.

**V**

They sailed to the Western Sea, they did,
　To a land all covered with trees,
And they bought an Owl, and a useful Cart,
And a pound of Rice, and a Cranberry Tart,
　And a hive of silvery Bees.
And they bought a Pig, and some green Jack-daws,
And a lovely Monkey with lollipop paws,
And forty bottles of Ring-Bo-Ree,
　And no end of Stilton Cheese.
　　Far and few, far and few,
　　　Are the lands where the Jumblies live;
　　Their heads are green, and their hands are blue,
　　　And they went to sea in a Sieve.

**VI**

And in twenty years they all came back,
　In twenty years or more,
And everyone said, "How tall they've grown!
For they've been to the Lakes, and the Torrible Zone,
　And the hills of the Chankly Bore";
And they drank their health, and gave them a feast
Of dumplings made of beautiful yeast;
And everyone said, "If we only live,
We too will go to sea in a Sieve, —
　To the hills of the Chankly Bore!"
　　Far and few, far and few,
　　　Are the lands where the Jumblies live;
　　Their heads are green, and their hands are blue,
　　　And they went to sea in a Sieve.

*Edward Lear*

## The Parent

Children aren't happy with nothing to ignore,
And that's what parents were created for.

Ogden Nash

49

From:

# The Rime of the Ancient Mariner

The fair breeze blew, the white foam flew,
   The furrow followed free;
We were the first that ever burst
   Into that silent sea.

Down dropt the breeze, the sails dropt down,
   'Twas sad as sad could be;
And we did speak only to break
   The silence of the sea!

All in a hot and copper sky
   The bloody sun, at noon,
Right up above the mast did stand,
   No bigger than the moon.

Day after day, day after day,
   We stuck, nor breath nor motion;
As idle as a painted ship
   Upon a painted ocean.

Water, water, everywhere,
   And all the boards did shrink;
Water, water, everywhere,
   Nor any drop to drink.

The very deep did rot: O Christ!
   That ever this should be!
Yea, slimy things did crawl with legs
   Upon the slimy sea.

About, about, in reel and rout
   The death-fires danced at night;
The water, like a witch's oils,
   Burnt green, and blue, and white.

And some in dreams assurèd were
   Of the spirit that plagued us so;
Nine fathom deep he had followed us
   From the land of mist and snow.

And every tongue, through utter drought,
   Was withered at the root;
We could not speak, no more than if
   We had been choked with soot.

Ah! Well-a-day! what evil looks
   Had I from old and young!
Instead of the cross, the Albatross
   About my neck was hung.

*Samuel Taylor Coleridge*

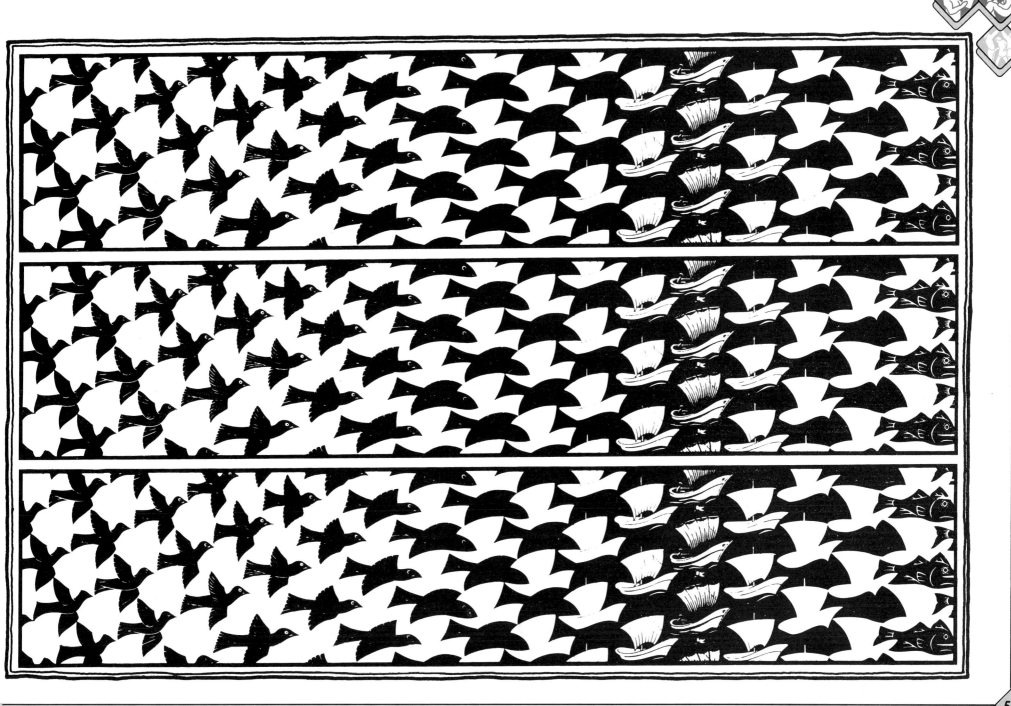

## Stopping by Woods on a Snowy Evening

Whose woods these are I think I know.
His house is in the village though;
He will not see me stopping here
To watch his woods fill up with snow.

My little horse must think it queer
To stop without a farmhouse near
Between the woods and frozen lake
The darkest evening of the year.

He gives his harness bells a shake
To ask if there is some mistake.
The only other sound's the sweep
Of easy wind and downy flake.

The woods are lovely, dark and deep,
But I have promises to keep,
And miles to go before I sleep,
And miles to go before I sleep.

*Robert Frost*

# Loveliest of Trees

Loveliest of trees, the cherry now
Is hung with bloom along the bough,
And stands about the woodland ride
Wearing white for Eastertide.

Now, of my threescore years and ten,
Twenty will not come again,
And take from seventy springs a score,
It only leaves me fifty more.

And since to look at things in bloom
Fifty springs are little room,
About the woodlands I will go
To see the cherry hung with snow.

*A. E. Housman*

From:

# The Prelude *Book 1*

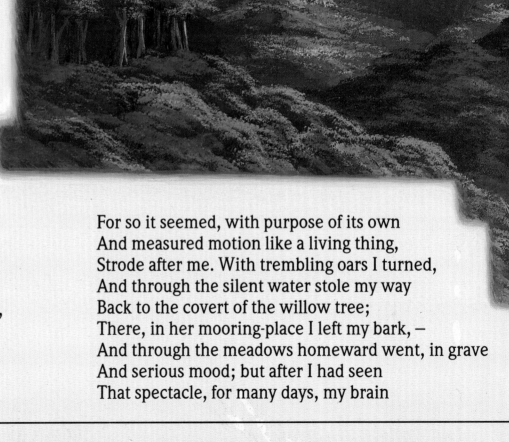

One summer evening (led by her) I found
A little boat tied to a willow tree
Within a rocky cave, its usual home.
Straight I unloosed her chain, and stepping in
Pushed from the shore. It was an act of stealth
And troubled pleasure, nor without the voice
Of mountain-echoes did my boat move on;
Leaving behind her still, on either side,
Small circles glittering idly in the moon,
Until they melted all into one track
Of sparkling light. But now, like one who rows,
Proud of his skill, to reach a chosen point
With an unswerving line, I fixed my view
Upon the summit of a craggy ridge,
The horizon's utmost boundary; for above
Was nothing but the stars and the grey sky.
She was an elfin pinnace; lustily
I dipped my oars into the silent lake,
And, as I rose upon the stroke, my boat
Went heaving through the water like a swan;
When, from behind that craggy steep till then
The horizon's bound, a huge peak, black and huge,
As if with voluntary power instinct
Upreared its head. I struck and struck again,
And growing still in stature the grim shape
Towered up between me and the stars, and still,

For so it seemed, with purpose of its own
And measured motion like a living thing,
Strode after me. With trembling oars I turned,
And through the silent water stole my way
Back to the covert of the willow tree;
There, in her mooring-place I left my bark, —
And through the meadows homeward went, in grave
And serious mood; but after I had seen
That spectacle, for many days, my brain

Worked with a dim and undetermined sense
Of unknown modes of being; o'er my thoughts
There hung a darkness, call it solitude
Or blank desertion. No familiar shapes
Remained, no pleasant images of trees,
Of sea or sky, no colours of green fields;
But huge and mighty forms, that do not live
Like living men, moved slowly through the mind
By day, and were a trouble to my dreams.

*William Wordsworth*

From:

# The Garden in September

Now thin mists temper the slow-ripening beams
Of the September sun: his golden gleams
On gaudy flowers shine, that prank the rows
Of high-grown hollyhocks, and all tall shows
That Autumn flaunteth in his bushy bowers;
Where tomtits, hanging from the drooping heads
Of giant sunflowers, peck the nutty seeds;
And in the feathery aster bees on wing
Seize and set free the honied flowers,
Till thousand stars leap with their visiting:
While ever across the path mazily flit,
Unpiloted in the sun,
The dreamy butterflies
With dazzling colours powdered and soft glooms,
White, black and crimson stripes, and peacock eyes,
Or on chance flowers sit,
With idle effort plundering one by one
The nectaries of deepest-throated blooms.

*Robert Bridges*

## Granny Granny Please Comb My Hair

Granny Granny
please comb my hair
you always take your time
you always take such care

You put me to sit on a cushion
between your knees
you rub a little coconut oil
parting gentle as a breeze

Mummy Mummy
she's always in a hurry – hurry
rush
she pulls my hair
sometimes she tugs

But Granny
you have all the time in the world
and when you're finished
you always turn my head and say
"Now who's a nice girl."

Grace Nichols

## Up the Stairs

My mum comes up the stairs plod, plod, plodding
Slowly, unmistakably.

My dad comes up fast
Often two at a time,
Heavily.

My brother tries to get up as quickly as possible.
What a noise he makes!
"More haste, less speed!"

He's the same coming down,
Rush, Rush, Rush!

I always jump the last step.

Simon Vincent (Aged 9)

## A Case of Murder

They should not have left him there alone,
Alone that is except for the cat.
He was only nine, not old enough
To be left alone in a basement flat,
Alone, that is, except for the cat.
A dog would have been a different thing,
A big gruff dog with slashing jaws,
But a cat with round eyes mad as gold,
Plump as a cushion with tucked-in paws –
Better have left him with a fair-sized rat!
But what they did was leave him with a cat.
He hated that cat; he watched it sit,
A buzzing machine of soft black stuff,
He sat and watched and he hated it,
Snug in its fur, hot blood in a muff,
And its mad gold stare and the way it sat
Crooning dark warmth: he loathed all that.
So he took Daddy's stick and he hit the cat.
Then quick as a sudden crack in glass
It hissed, black flash, to a hiding place
In the dust and dark beneath the couch,
And he followed the grin on his new-made face,
A wide-eyed, frightened snarl of a grin,
And he took the stick and he thrust it in,
Hard and quick in the furry dark,
The black fur squealed and he felt his skin
Prickle with sparks of dry delight.

Then the cat again came into sight,
Shot for the door that wasn't quite shut,
But the boy, quick too, slammed fast the door:
The cat, half-through, was cracked like a nut
And the soft black thud was dumped on the floor.
Then the boy was suddenly terrified
And he bit his knuckles and cried and cried;
But he had to do something with the dead
      thing there.
His eyes squeezed beads of salty prayer
But the wound of fear gaped wide and raw;
He dared not touch the thing with his hands
So he fetched a spade and shovelled it
And dumped the load of heavy fur
In the spidery cupboard under the stair
Where it's been for years, and though it died
It's grown in that cupboard and its hot low purr
Grows slowly louder year by year:
There'll not be a corner for the boy to hide
When the cupboard swells and all sides split
And the huge black cat pads out of it.

*Vernon Scannell*

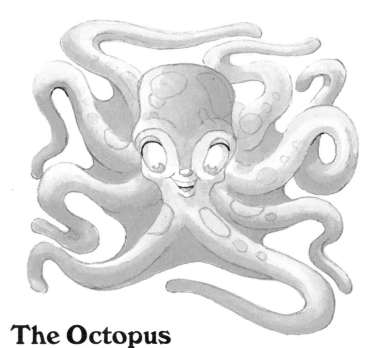

## The Octopus

Tell me, O Octopus, I begs,
Is those things arms, or is they legs?
I marvel at thee, Octopus;
If I were thou, I'd call me Us.

**Ogden Nash**

# A Poison Tree

I was angry with my friend:
I told my wrath, my wrath did end.
I was angry with my foe:
I told it not, my wrath did grow.

And I water'd it in fears,
Night and morning with my tears;
And I sunned it with smiles,
And with soft deceitful wiles.

And it grew both day and night,
Till it bore an apple bright;
And my foe beheld it shine,
And he knew that it was mine,

And into my garden stole
When the night had veil'd the pole:
In the morning glad I see
My foe outstretch'd beneath the tree.

*William Blake*

## A Thought

When I look into a glass,
  Myself's my only care;
But I look into a pool
  For all the wonders there.

When I look into a glass,
  I see a fool:
But I see a wise man
  When I look into a pool.

*W. H. Davies*

# She Walks in Beauty

She walks in beauty, like the night
    Of cloudless climes and starry skies;
And all that's best of dark and bright
    Meet in her aspect and her eyes:
Thus mellow'd to that tender light
    Which heaven to gaudy day denies.

One shade the more, one ray the less,
    Had half impair'd the nameless grace
Which waves in every raven tress,
    Or softly lightens o'er her face;
Where thoughts serenely sweet express
    How pure, how dear their dwelling-place.

And on that cheek, and o'er that brow,
    So soft, so calm, yet eloquent,
The smiles that win, the tints that glow,
    But tell of days in goodness spent,
A mind at peace with all below,
    A heart whose love is innocent!

*Lord Byron*

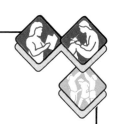

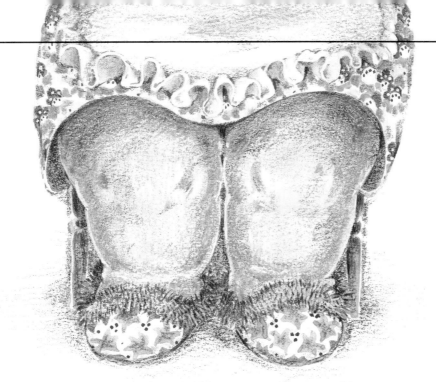

## Aunt Flo'

Was like a dumpling on legs, with a face as gentle
With colour and wrinkles as a stored pippin,
Her flesh rich and as yeasty as fresh bread.
When she served dinner we would all rush
For the far end of the long table,
The plates passed down as she overwhelmed them
With potatoes, meat, gravy and greens
Until the dishes and tureens were empty.
"Oh dear," she would say to those who sat near her,
"There's none left for you!"
Then the ritual was to be sent to the kitchen for
    cheese
And a cottage loaf which prompted me to wonder
Did the baker use her as a model?

Strictly teetotal, she sustained her abstinence
On Wincarnis and home-made wines.
"It's good for you," she would say
To nephews and nieces, "it's natural."
While mothers winced to see their young ones
    reeling away,
And her more sophisticated daughters
Recoiled at her too obvious refusal
To wear underclothes in warm weather.

Delectably dotty, Aunt Flo'
Blundered beautifully through life
And taught us, when, later,
In despair of making sense of things,
That it didn't matter.

*John Cotton*

From:

# Spring

Nothing is so beautiful as Spring –
    When weeds, in wheels, shoot long and lovely and lush;
    Thrush's eggs look little low heavens, and thrush
Through the echoing timber does so rinse and wring
The ear, it strikes like lightnings to hear him sing;
    The glassy peartree leaves and blooms, they brush
    The descending blue; that blue is all in a rush
With richness; the racing lambs too have fair their fling.

*Gerard Manley Hopkins*

# Birds' Nests

The summer nests uncovered by autumn wind,
Some torn, others dislodged, all dark,
Everyone sees them: low or high in tree,
Or hedge, or single bush, they hang like a mark.

Since there's no need of eyes to see them with
I cannot help a little shame
That I missed most, even at eye's level, till
The leaves blew off and made the seeing no game.

'Tis a light pang. I like to see the nests
Still in their places, now first known,
At home and by far roads. Boys knew them not,
Whatever jays and squirrels may have done.

And most I like the winter nests deep-hid
That leaves and berries fell into:
Once a dormouse dined there on hazel-nuts,
And grass and goose-grass seeds found soil and grew.

*Edward Thomas*

## Incident at West Bay

He drove on to the quay.
His children, Mark and Jane,
Shrilled their needs:
A ride in a boat for Mark,
Ice-cream and the sands for Jane.

Gulls banked and glided over
The nudging dinghies; waves
Mildly admonished
The walls with small slaps.
It was the first day of the holidays.

"Wait there," he said, "I'll bring
Ice-cream." Out of the car
He felt the breeze
Easing the vehemence of the sun.
He said, "I won't be long."

He walked a few steps before
He was hit by a shout; he spun
Quickly round
To see his car begin
To move to the edge of the quay.

It was blind; it could not see.
It did not hesitate
But toppled in.
The sea was shocked, threw up
Astonished lace-cuffed waves.

He ran, he followed, plunged,
And in the shifting green gloom
He saw the car's
Tipped shape; he clutched handle, lugged.
His lungs bulged, punishing.

Through glass he saw their faces
Float, eyes wide as hunger,
Staring mouths,
Their lost and sightless hands.
In his chest the sea heaved

And pressed, swelled black and burst
Flooding his skull; it dragged
Him up to air.
They hauled him out and spread him
Oozing on the slimed stone.

They pumped the salt and darkness
From his lungs and skull;
Light scoured his eyes.
The sun said, "Rise." The gulls
Fell silent, then echoed his long torn yell.

Vernon Scannell

## This is Just to Say

I have eaten
the plums
that were in
the icebox

and which
you were probably
saving
for breakfast

Forgive me
they were delicious
so sweet
and so cold

*William Carlos Williams*

# Grandad

Wrinkles across his face,
Glasses over his eyes,
White hair out of place,
That's my lovely Grandad.

Tells you a story
Of when he was a lad,
All those years ago,
That's my Grandad.

Fifty pence to spend,
Some sweets to eat
Perhaps a comic or two
That's my kind Grandad.

At the end of the day,
When it's time to go home,
We always get good wishes
From my lovely Grandad.

*Sam Griffin* (Aged 9)

# Bingo

B.I.N.G.O.
My Nan goes to bingo –
64, 78, 93, 82.

B.I.N.G.O.
Sing hooray, hooray, hooray, today.
My Nan's won five pounds.

B.I.N.G.O.
Closing up time for bingo.
"Come on! Clear off!"

B.I.N.G.O.
"Bingo's over! Time to go!
Bingo's closed! Out you go!"

B.I.N.G.O.
B.I.N.G.O.
B.I.N.G.O.
Bingo.

*Corrine Willson* (Aged 9)

## When You Are Old

When you are old and grey and full of sleep,
And nodding by the fire, take down this book,
And slowly read, and dream of the soft look
Your eyes had once, and of their shadows deep;

How many loved your moments of glad grace,
And loved your beauty with love false or true,
But one man loved the pilgrim soul in you,
And loved the sorrows of your changing face;

And bending down beside the glowing bars,
Murmur, a little sadly, how Love fled
And paced upon the mountains overhead
And hid his face amid a crowd of stars.

*W. B. Yeats*

## Grandma

Gone to the dead
Is a terrible thing
For you cannot
Dance and sing.

All the time
You have to lie.
It is a terrible thing
To die.

In the grave
You have to go.
I'd hate to die
Oh no, no, no.

*Susan Boughtwood* (Aged 8)

## Macavity: the Mystery Cat

Macavity's a Mystery Cat: he's called the Hidden Paw —
For he's the master criminal who can defy the Law.
He's the bafflement of Scotland Yard, the Flying Squad's despair:
For when they reach the scene of crime — *Macavity's not there!*

Macavity, Macavity, there's no one like Macavity,
He's broken every human law, he breaks the law of gravity.
His powers of levitation would make a fakir stare,
And when you reach the scene of crime — *Macavity's not there!*
You may seek him in the basement, you may look up in the air —
But I tell you once and once again, *Macavity's not there!*

Macavity's a ginger cat, he's very tall and thin;
You would know him if you saw him, for his eyes are sunken in.
His brow is deeply lined with thought, his head is highly domed;
His coat is dusty from neglect, his whiskers are uncombed.
He sways his head from side to side, with movements like a snake;
And when you think he's half asleep, he's always wide awake.

Macavity, Macavity, there's no one like Macavity,
For he's a fiend in feline shape, a monster of depravity.
You may meet him in a by-street, you may see him in the square —
But when a crime's discovered, then *Macavity's not there!*

He's outwardly respectable. (They say he cheats at cards.)
And his footprints are not found in any file of Scotland Yard's.
And when the larder's looted, or the jewel-case is rifled,
Or when the milk is missing
Or the greenhouse glass is broken, and the trellis past repair —
Ay, there's the wonder of the thing! *Macavity's not there!*

And when the Foreign Office find a Treaty's gone astray,
Or the Admiralty lose some plans and drawings by the way,
There may be a scrap of paper in the hall or on the stair —
But it's useless to investigate — *Macavity's not there!*
And when the loss has been disclosed, the Secret Service say:
"It *must* have been Macavity!" — but he's a mile away.
You'll be sure to find him resting, or a-licking of his thumbs,
Or engaged in doing complicated long division sums.

Macavity, Macavity, there's no one like Macavity,
There never was a Cat of such deceitfulness and suavity.
He always has an alibi, and one or two to spare:
At whatever time the deed took place — MACAVITY WASN'T THERE!
And they say that all the Cats whose wicked deeds are widely
     known
(I might mention Mungojerrie, I might mention Griddlebone)
Are nothing more than agents for the Cat who all the time
Just controls their operations: the Napoleon of Crime!

*T. S. Eliot*

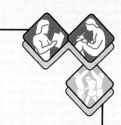

## The Pasture

I'm going out to clean the pasture spring;
I'll only stop to rake the leaves away
(And wait to watch the water clear, I may):
I shan't be gone long. — You come too.

I'm going out to fetch the little calf
That's standing by the mother. It's so young
It totters when she licks it with her tongue.
I shan't be gone long. — You come too.

*Robert Frost*

Have you been outside?
I have not. I said.
Then why are you wet?
I'm not. I said.
Then what are those drips?
What drips?
Those drips.
I've been playing in the water butt.
So you have been outside!

Simon Vincent (Aged 9)

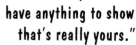

## Talking about reading and writing poetry

**Q.** "Do you ever read your own poems to yourself?"
**A.** "Yes, I keep reading them . . . I read one and *I remember* when I did this or that."

"Say I went on something at a fun-fair and I thought this is really exciting. I think when I get home, or at another time, I've definitely got to make a poem about it — I just think about it and make sure I've got it. If I think I'm enjoying myself too much, so I might not remember, I get a piece of paper out of my pocket and write it down, so when my mum washes my coat she takes all these bits of poems out."

"When you read lots of poems and listen to other peoples', I really find it helps to know how to write mine."

"It's very different when you are able to write at home as well as at school . . . the more time you get the more ideas you get."

"Writing does matter because it's interesting. It's important, it's fun, it makes you happy. You enjoy it when you have a choice, you can decide what you want to do."

"You can let your imagination run wild. I think it's important that you shouldn't always do what you're told in writing. I think you ought to be allowed to write what you want. If you don't, you'll find that you won't have anything to show that's really yours."

# Bibliography

◇ **Some poets and poems children often choose to read and listen to**

John Agard — *I Din Do Nuttin*, Bodley Head 1983
*Say It Again, Granny*, Bodley Head 1986

Allan Ahlberg — *Please Mrs. Butler*, Puffin 1984

Michael Baldwin — *Hob and other poems*, Chatto 1972

John Betjeman — *A Ring of Bells*, John Murray 1962

William Blake — *A Grain of Sand: poems for young readers chosen and introduced by Rosemary Manning*, Bodley Head 1967

Edmund Blunden — *The Midnight Skaters: poems for young readers chosen and introduced by C. Day Lewis*, Bodley Head 1968

Emily Bronte — *A Peculiar Music: poems for young children introduced by Naomi Lewis*, Bodley Head 1971

Alan Brownjohn — *Brownjohn's Beasts*, Macmillan 1970

Charles Causley — *Figgie Hobbin*, Puffin 1979
*Jack The Treacle Eater*, Macmillan 1987

John Clare — *The Wood is Sweet: poems for young readers chosen by David Powell*, Bodley Head 1966

Walter de la Mare — *Bells and Grass*, Faber 1941
*Peacock Pie*, Puffin 1962
*Secret Laughter*, Puffin 1972

T.S. Eliot — *Old Possum's Book of Practical Cats*, Faber 1974

Gavin Ewart — *The Learned Hippopotamus*, Hutchinson 1986

Max Fatchen — *Wry Rhymes for Troublesome Times*, Puffin 1985

Robert Frost — *You Come Too: favourite poems for young readers*, Bodley Head 1964

Roy Fuller — *Seen Grandpa Lately?* Andre Deutsch 1972
*Poor Roy*, Andre Deutsch 1977

Mick Gowar — *Swings and Roundabouts*, Collins 1981

John Heath-Stubbs — *A Parliament of Birds*, Chatto 1975

Robert Herrick — *The Music of a Feast: poems for young readers chosen by Eleanor Graham*, Bodley Head 1968

Phoebe Hesketh — *A Song of Sunlight*, Chatto 1974

Ted Hughes — *Meet My Folks*, Faber 1961
*Season Songs*, Faber 1976
*Moon Bells and other poems*, Chatto 1978
*What is the Truth?* Faber 1984

Elizabeth Jennings — *The Secret Brother and other poems for children*, Macmillan 1966

Brian Jones — *The Spitfire on the Northern Line*, Chatto 1975

Edward Lear — *A Book of Bosh: lyrics and prose of Edward Lear*, chosen by Brian Anderson, Kestrel 1975

*The Complete Nonsense of Edward Lear*, edited by Holbrook Jackson, Faber 1971

John Loveday — *Particular Sunlights*, Headland 1986

Gerda Mayer — *The Knockabout Show*, Chatto 1978

Roger McGough — *Sky in the Pie*, Puffin 1985

Roger McGough and Michael Rosen — *You Tell Me*, Puffin 1985

Spike Milligan — *Silly Verse for Kids*, Puffin 1974
*Goblins*, Hutchinson 1978
*Unspun Socks from a Chicken's Laundry*, Puffin 1982

Adrian Mitchell — *Nothingmas Day*, Allison and Busby 1984

John Mole — *Boo to a Goose*, Peterloo 1987

Ogden Nash — *Custard and Company*, Kestrel 1979

Judith Nicholls — *Midnight Forest*, Faber 1987

Gareth Owen — *Salford Road*, Macmillan 1984
*Song of the City*, Fontana Lion 1985

Brian Patten — *Gargling with Jelly*, Puffin 1986

Mervyn Peake — *A Book of Nonsense*, Peter Owen 1972

James Reeves — *Prefabulous Animiles*, Faber 1968

Michael Rosen — *Mind Your Own Business*, Fontana Lion 1974
*You Can't Catch Me*, Andre Deutsch 1981
*Wouldn't You Like to Know*, Puffin 1981
*Quick, Let's Get Out of Here*, Puffin 1985

Christina Rossetti — *Goblin Market,* Gollancz 1980

Clive Sansom — *An English Year,* Chatto 1975
Vernon Scannell — *The Apple Raid,* Chatto 1974
Shel Silverstein — *Uncle Shelby's Zoo,* Allen 1964
*A Light in the Attic,* Cape 1981
*Where the Sidewalk Ends,* Cape 1984

Edward Thomas — *The Green Roads: poems for young readers chosen by Eleanor Farjeon,* Bodley Head 1965
R.S. Thomas — *Young and Old,* Chatto 1972

Kit Wright — *Rabbitting On,* Fontana Lion 1978
*Hot Dog and other poems,* Puffin 1981

Andrew Young — *Burning as Light: 37 poems chosen by Leonard Clark,* Hart-Davis 1967
*Quiet as Moss: 36 poems chosen by Leonard Clark,* Hart-Davis 1967

Charlotte Zolotow — *River Winding,* World's Work 1980

## ◇ Some anthologies children often choose to read

*African Poetry for Schools* 1 and 2, ed. Noel Machin, Longman 1978
*All Sorts of Poems,* ed. Ann Thwaite, Methuen 1980
*All The Day Through,* ed. Wes Magee, Evans 1982

*The Batsford Book of Children's Verse,* ed. Gavin Ewart, Batsford 1976
*Beastly Boys and Ghastly Girls,* ed. William Cole, Methuen 1964

*The Children's Book of Funny Verse,* ed. Julie Watson, Faber 1979

*Days Are Where We Live,* ed. Jill Bennett, Bodley Head 1981
*Delights and Warnings,* ed. Gillian and John Beer, Macdonald 1979

*Evans Book of Children's Verse,* ed. Howard Sergeant, Evans 1972

*The Faber Book of Children's Verse,* ed. Janet Adams Smith, Faber 1973

*Ghosts, Gangsters and Dragonflies,* ed. Brian Patten, Allen and Unwin 1981

*I Like That Stuff,* ed. Morag Styles, Cambridge University Press 1984
*I'm Mad At You,* ed. William Cole, Collins 1978

*Junior Poetry Anthology,* Books 1-4, ed. Moira Andrew, Macmillan
  *The First Lick of the Lolly,* 1986
  *Marbles in my Pocket,* 1986
  *Go and Open the Door,* 1987
  *Unicorn and Lions,* 1987
*Junior Verses,* Books 1–4, ed. Geoffrey Summerfield, Penguin 1970

*The Kingfisher Book of Comic Verse,* ed. Roger McGough, Kingfisher Books 1986
*The Kingfisher Book of Poetry for Children,* ed. Michael Rosen, Kingfisher Books 1985

*Oh, How Silly!* ed. William Cole, Methuen 1971

*Oh, That's Ridiculous!* ed. William Cole, Methuen 1972
*Oh, What Nonsense!* ed. William Cole, Methuen 1968
*Over the Bridge,* ed. John Loveday, Puffin 1981
*The Oxford Book of Children's Verse,* eds. Iona and Peter Opie, Oxford University Press 1975
*The Oxford Book of Poetry for Children,* ed. Edward Blishen, Oxford University Press 1963

*A Packet of Poems,* ed. Jill Bennett, Oxford University Press 1982
*Poems for Nine and Under,* ed. Kit Wright, Puffin 1985
*Poems for Ten and Over,* ed. Kit Wright, Puffin 1985
*Poems That Go Bump in the Night,* eds. Zenka and Ian Woodward, Arrow 1985
*The Puffin Book of Magic Verse,* ed. Charles Causley, Penguin 1974
*The Puffin Book of Salt Sea Verse,* ed. Charles Causley, Penguin 1978

*The Rattle Bag,* eds. Seamus Heaney and Ted Hughes, Faber 1982
*Read Me A Poem,* ed. Caroline Royds, Kingfisher Books 1986

*Storm, and Other Old English Riddles,* ed. Kevin Crossley Holland, Macmillan 1970
*The Sun, Dancing,* ed. Charles Causley, Puffin 1984

*A Very First Poetry Book,* ed. John Foster, Oxford University Press 1984. Also *A First, Second, Third, Fourth* and *Fifth . . .* 1979, 1981, 1982, 1983, 1986

*The Walker Book of Poetry for Children,* ed. Jack Prelutsky, Walker Books 1983

*You'll Love This Stuff,* ed. Morag Styles, Cambridge University Press 1986

# Useful addresses and information

◇ **The National Poetry Centre**
21 Earls Court Square, London SW5 9DE
Tel: 01 373 7861/2

The Poetry Society has its headquarters at the above address and publishes a quarterly journal, *Poetry Review,* which is the major national journal devoted exclusively to poetry. The cost of membership of this society is modest, yet one of several attractive benefits is that members receive *Poetry Review* free. The society runs an excellent bookshop, and organizes a full programme of events and lectures connected with poetry.

Details of the society's work with teachers and children, including its administration of the *Poets in Schools* scheme, may be obtained from the *Education Officer,* at the above address.
Tel: 01 272 2551.

The *Poetry Book Society* is run from the same address.

◇ **Poetry Library South Bank Centre**
Royal Festival Hall, London SE1 8XX
Tel: 01 921 0664

Contains the most comprehensive collection of twentieth-century poetry in Great Britain.
Open seven days a week.

◇ **The Schools' Poetry Association**
27 Pennington Close, Colden Common, Near Winchester, Hampshire, SO21 1UR
Tel: 0962 712062

◇ **The Arvon Foundation** has centres at the following addresses:

*Arvon Foundation at Lumb Bank,* Heptonstall, Hebden Bridge, West Yorkshire HX7 6DF
Tel: 0422 843714

*Arvon Foundation at Totleigh Barton,* Totleigh Barton, Sheepwash, Devon EX21 5NS
Tel: 040 923 338

◇ The *Literature Officer* of your **regional arts association** may be contacted at one of these addresses:

## England

**Eastern Arts** (Bedfordshire, Cambridgeshire, Essex, Hertfordshire, Norfolk and Suffolk)
Cherry Hinton Hall, Cherry Hinton Rd, Cambridge CB1 4DW
Tel: 0223 215355

**East Midland Arts** (Derbyshire, excluding High Peak District, Leicestershire, Northamptonshire, Nottinghamshire and Buckinghamshire)
Mountfields House, Forest Rd, Loughborough, Leicestershire LE11 3HU
Tel: 0509 218292

**Greater London Arts** (the 32 London boroughs and the City of London)
9 White Lion St, London N1 9PD
Tel: 01 837 8808

**Lincolnshire & Humberside Arts** (Lincolnshire and Humberside)
St Hugh's, Newport, Lincoln LN1 3DN
Tel: 0522 33555

**Merseyside Arts** (Metropolitan County of Merseyside, District of West Lancashire, Ellesmere Port and Halton Districts of Cheshire)
Bluecoat Chambers, School La, Liverpool L1 3BX
Tel: 051 709 0671

**Northern Arts** (Cleveland, Cumbria, Durham, Northumberland, Metropolitan County of Tyne and Wear)
9–10 Osborne Terr, Newcastle upon Tyne NE2 1NZ
Tel: 091 281 6334

**North West Arts** (Greater Manchester, High Peak District of Derbyshire, Lancashire, except District of West Lancashire, and Cheshire, except Ellesmere Port and Halton Districts)
12 Harter St, Manchester M1 6HY
Tel: 061 228 3062

**Southern Arts** (Berkshire, Hampshire, Isle of Wight, Oxfordshire, West Sussex, Wiltshire, Districts of Bournemouth, Christchurch and Poole)
19 Southgate St, Winchester, Hampshire SO23 9DQ
Tel: 0962 55099

**South East Arts** (Kent, Surrey and East Sussex)
10 Mount Ephraim, Royal Tunbridge Wells, Kent TN4 8AS
Tel: 0892 515210

**South West Arts** (Avon, Cornwall, Devon, Dorset except Districts of Bournemouth, Christchurch and Poole, Gloucestershire and Somerset)
Bradninch Place, Gandy St, Exeter, Devon EX4 3LS
Tel: 0392 218188

**West Midlands Arts** (County of Hereford & Worcester, Metropolitan County of West Midlands, Shropshire, Staffordshire and Warwickshire)
82 Granville St, Birmingham B1 2LH
Tel: 021 631 3121

**Yorkshire Arts Association** (North Yorkshire, South Yorkshire and West Yorkshire)
Glyde House, Glydegate, Bradford, West Yorkshire BD5 0BQ
Tel: 0274 723051

# Wales

**North Wales Arts Association** (Clwyd, Gwynnedd and Montgomery)
10 Wellfield House, Bangor, Gwynnedd LL57 1ER
Tel: 0248 353248

**South East Wales Arts Association** (Gwent, Mid Glamorgan, South Glamorgan and Districts of Brecknock and Radnor in the County of Powys)
Victoria St, Cwmbran, Gwent NP44 3YT
Tel: 063 33 75075

**West Wales Association for the Arts** (Dyfed and West Glamorgan)
Dark Gate, Red St, Carmarthen, Dyfed SA31 1QL
Tel: 0267 234248

# Scotland and Ireland

Apply direct to the respective Arts Council:

**Scottish Arts Council**
19 Charlotte Square, Edinburgh EH2 4DF
Tel: 031 226 6051

**Arts Council of Northern Ireland**
181a Stranmillis Rd, Belfast BT9 5DU
Tel: 0232 381591

◇ **Arts Festivals in Britain and Ireland,** edited (1987/88 edition) by Sheena Barbour, is an invaluable reference book, full of information relevant to the teacher working in arts education. It is published by Rhinegold Publishers Ltd, London.

◇ **Tate Gallery**
Millbank, London SW1P 4RG
Tel: 01 821 1313

In recent years the Tate Gallery has been involved with teachers in encouraging children to develop their interest in writing poetry, alongside their education in the visual arts. Apply to the *Education Officer.*

# Index of titles* and authors

*\* Untitled poems are entered in this index under their first lines.*

# Index of first lines

# Acknowledgements

The publishers wish to thank the following for permission to reprint copyright poems in this volume. Every effort has been made to contact the owners of the copyright in these poems, but a few have proved impossible to locate. The publishers would be glad to hear from them so that correct acknowledgement can be made in future editions.

Anon: 'Apples are red' from *The Children's Book of Children's Rhymes* ed. Christopher Logue (B.T. Batsford), reprinted by permission of the publishers.

Anon: 'Little Miss Tuckett' from *The Puffin Book of Nursery Rhymes* ed. Iona and Peter Opie, reprinted by permission of Penguin Books Ltd.

Virginia Brasier: 'Psychological Prediction' reprinted by permission of The New Yorker Magazine, Inc, © 1942, 1970 The New Yorker Magazine.

Alan Brownjohn: 'Parrot' from *Brownjohn's Beasts,* reprinted by permission of Macmillan, London and Basingstoke.

Charles Causley: 'I Saw a Jolly Hunter' and 'What Has Happened to Lulu?' from *Figgie Hobbin* (Macmillan), reprinted by permission of David Higham Associates Ltd.

Leonard Clark: 'Dead and Alive' from *The Singing Time*, reprinted by permission of Hodder & Stoughton Ltd.

John Cotton: 'Aunt Flo' from *Oh Those Happy Feet* (Poet and Printer Press), © John Cotton, reprinted by permission of the author.

W. H. Davies: 'A Thought' from *The Complete Poems of W. H. Davies* (Jonathan Cape Ltd), reprinted by permission of the publishers and the Executors of the W. H. Davies Estate.

T. S. Eliot: 'Macavity: the Mystery Cat' reprinted by permission of Faber & Faber Ltd from *Old Possum's Book of Practical Cats.*

Robert Frost: 'Stopping by Woods on a Snowy Evening' and 'The Pasture' from *The Poetry of Robert Frost* ed. Edward Connery Latham (Jonathan Cape Ltd), reprinted by permission of the Estate of Robert Frost.

Martin Gardner: 'Magic Word' from *Never Make Fun of a Turtle My Son* reprinted by permission of the author.

Mary Ann Hoberman: 'Brother' from *Hello and Good-by* (Little Brown Inc), © 1959, renewed 1987 by Mary Ann Hoberman, reprinted by permission of Gina Maccoby Literary Agency.

Lucy Hosegood: 'Starlings' from *Those First Affections* by T.

Rodgers, reprinted by permission of Routledge & Kegan Paul Plc.

James Kirkup: 'Baby's Drinking Song' reprinted by permission of the author.

John Loveday: 'Children's Questions' from *Particular Sunlights* (Headland Publications 1986) and 'The Well' first published in *Over the Bridge* (Penguin Books Ltd 1981) and also published in *Particular Sunlights,* both poems © John Loveday, reprinted by permission of the author.

Spike Milligan: 'Fred Fernackerpan: A Mystery Goblin' from *Goblins,* reprinted by permission of Century Hutchinson Publishing Group Ltd; and 'Questions, Quistions and Quoshtions' from *The Little Potboiler,* reprinted by permission of W. H. Allen & Co Plc.

Ogden Nash: 'The Adventures of Isabel' from *The Bad Parents Garden of Verse* (Simon & Schuster), copyright © 1936, 1963 by Ogden Nash; 'The Octopus' from *Good Intentions,* copyright © 1942 by Ogden Nash; 'The Parent' from *Happy Days* (Little Brown 1933), copyright © 1933 by Ogden Nash; 'The Tale of Custard the Dragon' from *Happy Days* (Little Brown 1933), copyright © 1933 by Ogden Nash; all reprinted by permission of Curtis Brown Ltd; 'The Kitten' from *Custard and Company* (Kestrel Books 1979), copyright © 1979 by the Estate of Ogden Nash and Quentin Blake, reprinted by permission of Penguin Books Ltd.

Grace Nichols: 'Granny Granny Please Comb My Hair' © Grace Nichols, reprinted by permission of Curtis Brown Ltd on behalf of Grace Nichols.

Mervyn Peake: 'I Cannot Give the Reasons' from *A Book of Nonsense* (Peter Owen, London), reprinted by permission of the publishers.

Laura E. Richards: 'Eletelephony' from *Tirra Lirra: Rhymes Old and New,* copyright 1932 by Laura E. Richards, copyright renewed 1960 by Hamilton Richards, reprinted by permission of Little, Brown and Company.

Michael Rosen: 'Chivvy' from *You Tell Me* by Roger McGough and Michael Rosen (Kestrel Books, 1979) © Michael Rosen 1979, reprinted by permission of Penguin Books Ltd; 'I saw a lady with red hair' from *Mind Your Own Business* (Andre Deutsch 1974), reprinted by permission of Andre Deutsch.

Vernon Scannell: 'A Case of Murder' and 'Incident at West Bay' reprinted by permission of the author.

Shel Silverstein: 'Rain' from *Where the Sidewalk Ends,* reprinted by permission of Jonathan Cape Ltd.

Arnold Spilka: 'I Saw a Little Girl I Hate' from *A Rumbudgin of Nonsense,* by Arnold Spilka. Copyright © 1970 by Arnold Spilka. Reprinted by permission of Marian Reiner for the author.

Edward Thomas: 'Birds' Nests' from *Collected Poems* (Faber & Faber Ltd) reprinted by permission of Mrs Myfanwy Thomas.

William Carlos Williams: 'This is Just to Say' from *The Collected Poems 1909–1939* ed. A. Walton Litz and Christopher MacGowan (Carcanet Press Ltd), reprinted by permission of the publishers.

Kit Wright: 'It's Winter, It's Winter' from *Hot Dog and Other Poems* (Kestrel Books 1981) © Kit Wright 1981, reprinted by permission of Penguin Books Ltd; 'My Dad, Your Dad' from *Rabbiting On* (Young Lions, an imprint of the Collins Group) © Kit Wright 1978, reprinted by permission of the publishers.

W. B. Yeats: 'When You Are Old' from *The Collected Poems of W. B. Yeats,* reprinted by permission of A. P. Watt Ltd on behalf of Michael B. Yeats and Macmillan London Ltd.

Charlotte Zolotow: 'How Strange', 'In Bed' and 'Little Old Man' from *River Winding,* reproduced with the permission of Blackie and Son Ltd, Glasgow and London.

The following poems are published for the first time in this anthology and appear by permission of their authors:

Anjuna Dharni: 'The Check-up' and 'What's for Tea?'
Sam Griffin: 'Grandad'
Linda Huff: 'My Hospital Visit'
Simon Vincent: 'Have you been outside?', 'Up the Stairs', 'Where do pineapples grow?' and 'Yogurt Pots'
Corrine Willson: 'Bingo' and 'The Sulk'

Illustration acknowledgement
The illustration on page 51, 'Metamorphose III (Part IV)' by M. C. Escher, is © 1988 M. C. Escher c/o Cordon Art, Baarn, Holland.